HISTORIA CALAMITATUM AND THE LETTERS OF ABELARD AND HELOISE

PETER ABELARD

FV Editions

Contents

HISTORIA CALAMITATUM

LETTERS OF ABELARD AND HELOISE

HISTORIA CALAMITATUM
THE STORY OF MY MISFORTUNES

Introduction

The "Historia Calamitatum" of Peter Abélard is one of those human documents, out of the very heart of the Middle Ages, that illuminates by the glow of its ardour a shadowy period that has been made even more dusky and incomprehensible by unsympathetic commentators and the ill-digested matter of "source-books." Like the "Confessions" of St. Augustine it is an authentic revelation of personality and, like the latter, it seems to show how unchangeable is man, how consistent unto himself whether he is of the sixth century or the twelfth—or indeed of the twentieth century. "Evolution" may change the flora and fauna of the world, or modify its physical forms, but man is always the same and the unrolling of the centuries affects him not at all. If we can assume the vivid personality, the enormous intellectual power and the clear, keen mentality of Abélard and his contemporaries and immediate successors, there is no reason why "The Story of My Misfortunes" should not have been written within the last decade.

They are large assumptions, for this is not a period in world history when the informing energy of life expresses itself through such qualities, whereas the twelfth century was of precisely this nature. The antecedent hundred years had seen the recovery from the barbarism that engulfed Western Europe after the fall of Rome, and the generation of those vital forces that for two centuries were to infuse society with a vigour almost unexampled in its potency and in the things it brought to pass. The parabolic curve that describes the trajectory of Mediaevalism was then emergent out of "chaos and old night" and Abélard and his opponent, St. Bernard, rode high on the mounting force in its swift and almost violent ascent.

Pierre du Pallet, yclept Abélard, was born in 1079 and died in 1142, and his life precisely covers the period of the birth, development and perfecting of that Gothic style of architecture which is one of the great exemplars of the period. Actually, the Norman development occupied the years from 1050 to 1125 while the initiating and determining of Gothic consumed only fifteen years, from Bury, begun in 1125, to Saint-Denis, the work of Abbot Suger, the friend and partisan of Abélard, in 1140. It was the time of the Crusades, of the founding and development of schools and universities, of the invention or recovery of great arts, of the growth of music, poetry and romance. It was the age of great kings and knights and leaders of all kinds, but above all it was the epoch of a new philosophy, refounded on the newly revealed corner stones of Plato and Aristotle, but with a new content, a new impulse and a new method inspired by Christianity.

All these things, philosophy, art, personality, character, were the product of the time, which, in its definiteness and consistency, stands apart from all other epochs in history. The social system was that of feudalism, a scheme of reciprocal duties, privileges and obligations as between man and man that has never been excelled by any other system that society has developed as its own method of operation. As Dr. De Wulf has said in his illuminating book "Philosophy and Civilization in the Middle Ages" (a volume that should be read by any one who wishes rightly to understand the spirit and quality of Mediaevalism), "the feudal sentiment *par excellence* ... is the sentiment of the value and dignity of the individual man. The feudal man lived as a free man; he was master in his own house; he sought his end in himself; he was— and this is a scholastic expression,—*propter seipsum existens*: all feudal obligations were founded upon respect for personality and the given word."

Of course this admirable scheme of society with its guild system of industry, its absence of usury in any form and its just sense of comparative values, was shot through and through with religion both in faith and practice. Catholicism was universally and implicitly accepted. Monasticism had redeemed Europe from barbarism and Cluny had freed the Church from the yoke of German imperialism. This unity and immanence of religion gave a consistency to society otherwise unobtainable, and poured its vitality into every form of human thought and action.

It was Catholicism and the spirit of feudalism that preserved men from the dangers inherent in the immense individualism of the time. With this powerful and penetrating coördinating force men were safe to go about as far as they liked in the line of individuality, whereas today, for example, the unifying force of a common and vital religion being absent and nothing having been offered to take its place, the result of a similar tendency is egotism and anarchy. These things happened in the end in the case of Mediaevalism when the power and the influence of religion once began to weaken, and the Renaissance and Reformation dissolved the fabric of a unified society. Thereafter it became necessary to bring some order out of the spiritual, intellectual and physical chaos through the application of arbitrary force, and so came absolutism in government, the tyranny of the new intellectualism, the Catholic Inquisition and the Puritan Theocracy.

In the twelfth and thirteenth centuries, however, the balance is justly preserved, though it was but an unstable equilibrium, and therefore during the time of Abélard we find the widest diversity of speculation and freedom of thought which continue unhampered for more than a hundred years. The mystical school of the Abbey of St. Victor in Paris follows one line (perhaps the most nearly right of all though it was submerged by the intellectual force and vivacity of the Scholastics) with Hugh of St. Victor as its greatest exponent. The Franciscans and Dominicans each possessed great schools of philosophy and dogmatic theology, and in addition there were a dozen individual line of speculation, each vitalized by some one personality, daring, original, enthusiastic. This prodigious mental and spiritual activity was largely fostered by the schools, colleges and universities that had suddenly appeared all over Europe. Never was such activity along educational lines. Almost every cathedral had its school, and many of the abbeys as well, as for example, in France alone, Cluny, Citeaux and Bec, St. Martin of Tours, Laon, Chartres, Rheims and Paris. To these schools students poured in from all over the world in numbers mounting to many thousands for such as Paris for example, and the mutual rivalries were intense and sometimes disorderly. Groups of students would choose their own

masters and follow them from place to place, even subjecting them to
discipline if in their opinion they did not live up to the intellectual
mark they had set as their standard. As there was not only one religion
and one social system, but one universal language as well, this gathering from all the four quarters of Europe was perfectly possible, and
had much to do with the maintenance of that unity which marked
society for three centuries.

At the time of Abélard the schools of Chartres and Paris were at
the height of their fame and power. Fulbert, Bernard and Thierry, all of
Chartres, had fixed its fame for a long period, and at Paris Hugh and
Richard of St. Victor and William of Champeaux were names to
conjure with, while Anselm of Laon, Adelard of Bath, Alan of Lille,
John of Salisbury, Peter Lombard, were all from time to time students
or teachers in one of the schools of the Cathedral, the Abbey of St.
Victor or Ste. Geneviève.

Earlier in the Middle Ages the identity of theology and philosophy
had been proclaimed, following the Neo-Platonic and Augustinian
theory, and the latter (cf. Peter Damien and Duns Scotus Eriugena) was
even reduced to a position that made it no more than the obedient
handmaid of theology. In the eleventh century however, St. Anselm
had drawn a clear distinction between faith and reason, and thereafter
theology and philosophy were generally accepted as individual but
allied sciences, both serving as lines of approach to truth but differing
in their method. Truth was one and therefore there could be no
conflict between the conclusions reached after different fashions. In
the twelfth century Peter of Blois led a certain group called "rigourists"
who still looked askance at philosophy, or rather at the intellectual
methods by which it proceeded, and they were inclined to condemn it
as "the devil's art," but they were on the losing side and John of Salisbury, Alan of Lille, Gilbert de la Porrée and Hugh of St. Victor
prevailed in their contention that philosophers were "*humanae videlicet
sapientiae amatores*," while theologians were "_divinae scripturae
doctores."

Cardinal Mercier, himself the greatest contemporary exponent of
Scholastic philosophy, defines philosophy as "the science of the totality
of things." The twelfth century was a time when men were striving to
see phenomena in this sense and established a great rational synthesis
that should yet be in full conformity with the dogmatic theology of

revealed religion. Abélard was one of the most enthusiastic and daring of these Mediaeval thinkers, and it is not surprising that he should have found himself at issue not only with the duller type of theologians but with his philosophical peers themselves. He was an intellectual force of the first magnitude and a master of dialectic; he was also an egotist through and through, and a man of strong passions. He would and did use his logical faculty and his mastery of dialectic to justify his own desires, whether these were for carnal satisfaction or the maintenance of an original intellectual concept. It was precisely this danger that aroused the fears of the "rigourists" and in the light of succeeding events in the domain of intellectualism it is impossible to deny that there was some justification for their gloomy apprehensions. In St. Thomas Aquinas this intellectualizing process marked its highest point and beyond there was no margin of safety. He himself did not overstep the verge of danger, but after him this limit was overpassed. The perfect balance between mind and spirit was achieved by Hugh of St. Victor, but afterwards the severance began and on the one side was the unwholesome hyper-spiritualization of the Rhenish mystics, on the other the false intellectualism of Descartes, Kant and the entire modern school of materialistic philosophy. It was the clear prevision of this inevitable issue that made of St. Bernard not only an implacable opponent of Abélard but of the whole system of Scholasticism as well. For a time he was victorious. Abélard was silenced and the mysticism of the Victorines triumphed, only to be superseded fifty years later when the two great orders, Dominican and Franciscan, produced their triumphant protagonists of intellectualism, Alelander Halesand Albertus Magnus, and finally the greatest pure intellect of all time, St. Thomas Aquinas. St. Bernard, St. Francis of Assisi, the Victorines, maintained that after all, as Henri Bergson was to say, seven hundred years later, "the mind of man by its very nature is incapable of apprehending reality," and that therefore faith is better than reason. Lord Bacon came to the same conclusion when he wrote "Let men please themselves as they will in admiring and almost adoring the human kind, this is certain; that, as an uneven mirrour distorts the rays of objects according to its own figure and section, so the mind ... cannot be trusted." And Hugh of St. Victor himself, had written, even in the days of Abélard: "There was a certain wisdom that seemed such to them that knew not the true wisdom. The world found it and began to be puffed up, thinking itself great in this. Confiding in its wisdom it became presumptuous and boasted it would attain the highest wisdom. And it made itself a ladder of the face of creation. ... Then those things which were seen were known and there were other things which were not known; and through those which were manifest they expected to reach those that were hidden. And they stumbled and fell into the falsehoods of their own imagining ... So God made foolish the wisdom of this world, and He pointed out another wisdom, which seemed foolishness and was not. For it preached Christ crucified, in order that truth might be sought in humility. But the world despised it, wishing to contemplate the works of God, which He had made a source of wonder, and it did not wish to venerate what He had set for imitation, neither did it look to its own disease, seeking medicine in piety; but presuming on a false health, it gave itself over with vain curiosity to the study of alien things."

These considerations troubled Abélard not at all. He was conscious of a mind of singular acuteness and a tongue of parts, both of which would do whatever he willed. Beneath all the tumultuous talk of Paris, when he first arrived there, lay the great and unsolved problem of Universals and this he promptly made his own, rushing in where others feared to tread. William of Champeaux had rested on a Platonic basis, Abélard assumed that of Aristotle, and the clash began. It is not a lucid subject, but the best abstract may be found in Chapter XIV of Henry Adams' "Mont-Saint-Michel and Chartres" while this and the two succeeding chapters give the most luminous and vivacious account of the principles at issue in this most vital of intellectual feuds.

"According to the latest authorities, the doctrine of universals which convulsed the schools of the twelfth century has never received an adequate answer. What is a species: what is a genus or a family or an order? More or less convenient terms of classification, about which the twelfth century cared very little, while it cared deeply about the essence of classes! Science has become too complex to affirm the existence of universal truths, but it strives for nothing else, and disputes the problem, within its own limits, almost as earnestly as in the twelfth century, when the whole field of human and superhuman activity was shut between these barriers of substance, universals, and particulars. Little has changed except the vocabulary and the method. The schools knew that their society hung for life on the demonstration that God, the ultimate universal, was a reality, out of which all other universal truths or realities sprang. Truth was a real thing, outside of human experience. The schools of Paris talked and thought of nothing else. John of Salisbury, who attended Abélard's lectures about 1136, and became Bishop of Chartres in 1176, seems to have been more surprised than we need be at the intensity of the emotion. 'One never gets away from this question,' he said. 'From whatever point a discussion starts, it is always led back and attached to that. It is the madness of Rufus about Naevia; "He thinks of nothing else; talks of nothing else, and if Naevia did not exist, Rufus would be dumb."'

... "In these scholastic tournaments the two champions started from opposite points:—one from the ultimate substance, God,—the universal, the ideal, the type;—the other from the individual, Socrates, the concrete, the observed fact of experience, the object of sensual perception. The first champion—William in this instance— assumed that the universal was a real thing; and for that reason he was called a realist. His opponent—Abélard—held that the universal was only nominally real; and on that account he was called a nominalist. Truth, virtue, humanity, exist as units and realities, said William. Truth, replied Abélard, is only the sum of all possible facts that are true, as humanity is the sum of all actual human beings. The ideal bed is a form, made by God, said Plato. The ideal bed is a name, imagined by ourselves, said Aristotle. 'I start from the universe,' said William. 'I start from the atom,' said Abélard; and, once having started, they necessarily came into collision at some point between the two."

In this "Story of My Misfortunes" Abélard gives his own account of the triumphant manner in which he confounded his master, William, but as Henry Adams says, "We should be more credulous than twelfth-century monks, if we believed, on Abélard's word in 1135, that in 1110 he had driven out of the schools the most accomplished dialectician of the age by an objection so familiar that no other dialectician was ever silenced by it—whatever may have been the case with theologians-and so obvious that it could not have troubled a scholar of fifteen. William stated a selected doctrine as old as Plato; Abélard interposed an objection as old as Aristotle. Probably Plato and Aristotle had received the question and answer from philosophers ten thousand years older than themselves. Certainly the whole of philosophy has always been involved in this dispute."

So began the battle of the schools with all its more than military strategy and tactics, and in the end it was a drawn battle, in spite of its marvels of intellectual heroism and dialectical sublety. Says Henry Adams again:—

"In every age man has been apt to dream uneasily, rolling from side to side, beating against imaginary bars, unless, tired out, he has sunk into indifference or scepticism. Religious minds prefer scepticism. The true saint is a profound sceptic; a total disbeliever in human reason, who has more than once joined hands on this ground with some who were at best sinners. Bernard was a total disbeliever in Scholasticism; so was Voltaire. Bernard brought the society of his time to share his scepticism, but could give the society no other intellectual amusement to relieve its restlessness. His crusade failed; his ascetic enthusiasm faded; God came no nearer. If there was in all France, between 1140 and 1200, a more typical Englishman of the future Church of England type than John of Salisbury, he has left no trace; and John wrote a description of his time which makes a picturesque contrast with the picture painted by Abélard, his old master, of the century at its beginning. John weighed Abélard and the schools against Bernard and the cloister, and coolly concluded that the way to truth led rather through Citeaux, which brought him to Chartres as Bishop in 1176, and to a mild scepticism in faith. 'I prefer to doubt' he said, 'rather than rashly define what is hidden.' The battle with the schools had then resulted only in creating three kinds of sceptics:— the disbelievers in human reason; the passive agnostics; and the sceptics proper, who would have been atheists had they dared. The first class was represented by the School of St. Victor; the second by John of Salisbury himself; the third, by a class of schoolmen whom he called Cornificii, as though they made a practice of inventing horns of dilemma on which to fix their opponents; as, for example, they asked whether a pig which was led to market was led by the man or the cord. One asks instantly: What cord? —Whether Grace, for instance, or Free Will?

"Bishop John used the science he had learned in the school only to reach the conclusion that, if philosophy were a science at all, its best practical use was to teach charity—love. Even the early, superficial debates of the schools, in 1100-50, had so exhausted the subject that the most intelligent men saw how little was to be gained by pursuing further those lines of thought. The twelfth century had already reached the point where the seventeenth century stood when Descartes renewed the attempt to give a solid, philosophical basis for deism by his celebrated '*Cogito, ergo sum.*' Although that ultimate fact seemed new to Europe when Descartes revived it as the starting-point of his demonstration, it was as old and familiar as St. Augustine to the twelfth century, and as little conclusive as any other assumption of the Ego or the Non-Ego. The schools argued, according to their tastes, from unity to multiplicity, or from multiplicity to unity; but what they wanted was to connect the two. They tried realism and found that it led to pantheism. They tried nominalism and found that it ended in materialism. They attempted a compromise in conceptualism which begged the whole question. Then they lay down, exhausted. In the seventeenth century—the same violent struggle broke out again, and wrung from Pascal the famous outcry of despair in which the French language rose, perhaps for the last time, to the grand style of the twelfth century. To the twelfth century it belongs; to the century of faith and simplicity; not to the mathematical certainties of Descartes and Leibnitz and Newton, or to the mathematical abstractions of Spinoza. Descartes had proclaimed his famous conceptual proof of God: 'I am conscious of myself, and must exist; I am conscious of God and He must exist.' Pascal wearily replied that it was not God he doubted, but logic. He was tortured by the impossibility of rejecting man's reason by reason; unconsciously sceptical, he forced himself to disbelieve in himself rather than admit a doubt of God. Man had tried to prove God, and had failed: 'The metaphysical proofs of God are so remote (*éloignées*) from the reasoning of men, and so contradictory (*impliquées*, far fetched) that they made little impression; and even if they served to convince some people, it would only be during the instant that they see the demonstration; an hour afterwards they fear to have deceived themselves.'"

Abélard was always, as he has been called, a scholastic adventurer, a philosophical and theological freelance, and it was after the Calamity that he followed those courses that resulted finally in his silencing and his obscure death. It is almost impossible for us of modern times to understand the violence of partisanship aroused by his actions and published words that centre apparently around the placing of the hermitage he had made for himself under the patronage of the third Person of the Trinity, the Paraclete, the Spirit of love and compassion and consolation, and the consequent arguments by which he justified himself. To us it seems that he was only trying to exalt the power of the Holy Spirit, a pious action at the least but to the episcopal and monastic conservators of the faith he seems to have been guilty of trying to rationalize an unsolvable mystery, to find an intellectual solution forbidden to man. In some obscure way the question seems to be involved in that other of the function of the Blessed Virgin as the fount of mercy and compassion, and at this time when the cult of the Mother of God had reached its highest point of potency and poignancy anything of the sort seemed intolerable.

For a time the affairs of Abélard prospered: Abbot Suger of Saint-Denis was his defender, and he enjoyed the favor of the Pope and the King. He was made an abbot and his influence spread in every direction. In 1137 the King died and conditions at Rome changed so that St. Bernard became almost Pope and King in his own person. Within a year he proceeded against Abélard; his "Theology" was condemned at a council of Sens, this judgment was confirmed by the Pope, and the penalty of silence was imposed on the author— probably the most severe punishment he could be called upon to endure. As a matter of fact it was fatal to him. He started forthwith for Rome but stopped at the Abbey of Cluny in the company of its Abbot, Peter the Venerable, "the most amiable figure of the twelfth century," and no very devoted admirer of St. Bernard, to whom, as a matter of fact, he had once written, "You perform all the difficult religious duties; you fast, you watch, you suffer; but you will not endure the easy ones-you do not love." Here he found two years of peace after his troubled life, dying in the full communion of the Church on 21 April, 1142.

The problems of philosophy and theology that were so vital in the Middle Ages interest us no more, even when they are less obscure than those so rife in the twelfth century, but the problem of human love is always near and so it is not perhaps surprising that the abiding interest concerns itself with Abélard's relationship with Héloïse. So far as he is concerned it is not a very savoury matter. He deliberately seduced a pupil, a beautiful girl entrusted to him by her uncle, a simpleminded old canon of the Cathedral of Paris, under whose roof he ensconced himself by false pretenses and with the full intention of gaining the niece for himself. Abélard seems to have exercised an irresistible fascination for men and women alike, and his plot succeeded to admiration.

Stricken by a belated remorse, he finally married Héloïse against her unselfish protests and partly to legitimatize his unborn child, and shortly after he was surprised and overpowered by emissaries of Canon Fulbert and subjected to irreparable mutilation. He tells the story with perfect frankness and with hardly more than formal expressions of compunction, and thereafter follows the narrative of their separation, he to a monastery, she to a convent, and of his care for her during her conventual life, or at least for that part of it that had passed before the "History" was written. Through the whole story it is Héloise who shines brightly as a curiously beautiful personality, unselfish, self sacrificing, and almost virginal in her purity in spite of her fault. One has for her only sympathy and affection whereas it is difficult to feel either for Abélard in spite of his belated efforts at rectifying his own sin and his life-long devotion to his solitary wife in her hidden cloister.

The whole story was instantly known, Abélard's assailants were punished in kind, .and he himself shortly resumed his work of lecturing on philosophy and, a little later, on theology. Apparently his reputation did not suffer in the least, nor did hers; in fact her piety became almost a by-word and his name as a great teacher increased by leaps and bounds: neither his offence nor its punishment seemed to bring lasting discredit. This fact, which seems strange to us, does not imply a lack of moral sense in the community but rather the prevalence of standards alien to our own. It is only since the advent of Puritanism that sexual sins have been placed at the head of the whole category. During the Middle Ages, as always under Christianity, the most deadly sins were pride, covetousness, slander and anger. These implied inherent moral depravity, but "illicit" love was love outside the law of man, and did not of necessity and always involve moral guilt. Christ was Himself very gentle and compassionate with the sins of the flesh but relentless in the case of the greater sins of the spirit. Puritanism overturned the balance of things, and by concentrating its condemnation on sexual derelictions became blind to the greater sins of pride, avarice and anger. We have inherited the prejudice without acquiring the abstention, but the Middle Ages had a clearer sense of comparative values and they could forgive, or even ignore, the sin of Abélard and Héloïse when they could less easily excuse the sin of spiritual pride or deliberate cruelty. Moreover, these same Middle Ages believed very earnestly in the Divine forgiveness of sins for which there had been real repentance and honest effort at amendment. Abélard and Héloise had been grievously punished, he himself had made every reparation that was possible, his penitence was charitably assumed, and therefore it was not for society to condemn what God would mercifully forgive.

The twelfth and thirteenth centuries were not an age of moral laxity; ideals and standards and conduct were immeasurably higher than they had been for five hundred years, higher than they were to be in the centuries that followed the crest of Mediaevalism. It was however a time of enormous vitality, of throbbing energy that was constantly bursting its bounds, and as well a time of personal liberty and freedom of action that would seem strange indeed to us in these days of endless legal restraint and inhibitions mitigated by revolt. There were few formal laws but there was *Custom* which was a sovereign law in itself, and above all there was the moral law of the Church, establishing its great fundamental principles but leaving details to the working out of life itself. Behind the sin of Abélard lay his intolerable spiritual pride, his selfishness and his egotism, qualities that society at large did not recognize because of their devotion to his engaging personality and their admiration for his dazzling intellectual gifts. Their idol had sinned, he had been savagely punished, he had repented; that was all there was about it and the question was at an end.

In reading the Historia Calamitatum there is one consideration that suggests itself that is subject for serious thought. Written as it was some years after the great tragedy of his life, it was a portrait that somehow seems out of focus. We know that during his early years in Paris Abélard was a bold and daring champion in the lists of dialectic; brilliant, persuasive, masculine to a degree; yet this self-portrait is of a man timid, suspicious, frightened of realities, shadows, possibilities. He is in abject terror of councils, hidden enemies, even of his life. The tone is querulous, even peevish at times, and always the egotism and the pride persist, while he seems driven by the whip of desire for intellectual adventure into places where he shrinks from defending himself, or is unable to do so. The antithesis is complete and one is driven to believe that the terrible mutilation to which he had been subjected had broken down his personality and left him in all things less than man. His narrative is full of accusations against all manner of people, but it is not necessary to take all these literally, for it is evident that his natural egotism, overlaid by the circumstances of his calamity, produced an almost pathological condition wherein suspicions became to him realities and terrors established facts.

It is doubtful if Abélard should be ranked very high in the list of Mediaeval philosophers. He was more a dialectician than a creative force, and until the development of the episode with Héloïse he seems to have cared primarily for the excitement of debate, with small regard for the value or the subjects under discussion. As an intellectualist he had much to do with the subsequent abandonment of Plato in favour of Aristotle that was a mark of pure scholasticism, while the brilliancy of his dialectical method became a model for future generations. Afer the Calamity he turned from philosophy to theology and ethics and here he reveals qualities of nobility not evident before. Particularly does he insist upon the fact that it is the subjective intention that determines the moral value of human actions even if it does not change their essential character.

The story of this philosophical soldier of fortune is a romance from beginning to end, a poignant human drama shot through with passion, adventure, pathos and tragedy. In a sense it is an epitome of the earlier Middle Ages and through it shines the bright light of an era of fervid living, of exciting adventure, of phenomenal intellectual force and of large and comprehensive liberty. As a single episode of passion it is not particularly distinguished except for the appealing personality of Héloïse; as a phase in the development of Christian philosophy it is of only secondary value. United in one, the two factors achieve a brilliant dramatic unity that has made the story of Abélard and Héloïse immortal.

Ralph Adams Cram

HISTORIA CALAMITATUM
FOREWORD

Often the hearts of men and women are stirred, as likewise they are soothed in their sorrows, more by example than by words. And therefore, because I too have known some consolation from speech had with one who was a witness thereof, am I now minded to write of the sufferings which have sprung out of my misfortunes, for the eyes of one who, though absent, is of himself ever a consoler. This I do so that, in comparing your sorrows with mine, you may discover that yours are in truth nought, or at the most but of small account, and so shall you come to bear them more easily.

OF THE BIRTHPLACE OF
PIERRE ABÉLARD AND OF HIS
PARENTS

Know, then, that I am come from a certain town which was built on the way into lesser Brittany, distant some eight miles, as I think, eastward from the city of Nantes, and in its own tongue called Palets. Such is the nature of that country, or, it may be, of them who dwell there—for in truth they are quick in fancy—that my mind bent itself easily to the study of letters. Yet more, I had a father who had won some smattering of letters before he had girded on the soldier's belt. And so it came about that long afterwards his love thereof was so strong that he saw to it that each son of his should be taught in letters even earlier than in the management of arms. Thus indeed did it come to pass. And because I was his first born, and for that reason the more dear to him, he sought with double diligence to have me wisely taught. For my part, the more I went forward in the study of letters, and ever more easily, the greater became the ardour of my devotion to them, until in truth I was so enthralled by my passion for learning that, gladly leaving to my brothers the pomp of glory in arms, the right of heritage and all the honours that should have been mine as the eldest born, I fled utterly from the court of Mars that I might win learning in the bosom of Minerva. And since I found the armory of logical reasoning more to my liking than the other forms of philosophy, I exchanged all other weapons for these, and to the prizes of victory in war I preferred the battle of minds in disputation. Thenceforth, journeying through many provinces, and debating as I went, going whithersoever I heard that the study of my chosen art most flourished, I became such an one as the Peripatetics.

OF THE PERSECUTION HE HAD FROM HIS MASTER WILLIAM OF CHAMPEAUX—OF HIS ADVENTURES AT MELUN, AT CORBEIL AND AT PARIS—OF HIS WITHDRAWAL FROM THE CITY OF THE PARISIANS TO MELUN, AND HIS RETURN TO MONT STE. GENEVIÈVE—OF HIS JOURNEY TO HIS OLD HOME

I came at length to Paris, where above all in those days the art of dialectics was most flourishing, and there did I meet William of Champeaux, my teacher, a man most distinguished in his science both by his renown and by his true merit. With him I remained for some time, at first indeed well liked of him; but later I brought him great grief, because I undertook to refute certain of his opinions, not infrequently attacking him in disputation, and now and then in these debates I was adjudged victor. Now this, to those among my fellow students who were ranked foremost, seemed all the more insufferable because of my youth and the brief duration of my studies.

Out of this sprang the beginning of my misfortunes, which have followed me even to the present day; the more widely my fame was spread abroad, the more bitter was the envy that was kindled against me. It was given out that I, presuming on my gifts far beyond the warranty of my youth, was aspiring despite my tender, years to the leadership of a school; nay, more, that I was making read the very place in which I would undertake this task, the place being none other than the castle of Melun, at that time a royal seat. My teacher himself had some foreknowledge of this, and tried to remove my school as far as possible from his own. Working in secret, he sought in every way he could before I left his following to bring to nought the school I had planned and the place I had chosen for it. Since, however, in that very place he had many rivals, and some of them men of influence among the great ones of the land, relying on their aid I won to the fulfillment of my wish; the support of many was secured for me by reason of his own unconcealed envy. From this small inception of my school, my fame in the art of dialectics began to spread abroad, so that little by little the renown, not alone of those who had been my fellow students, but of our very teacher himself, grew dim and was like to die out altogether. Thus it came about that, still more confident in myself, I moved my school as soon as I well might to the castle of Corbeil, which is hard by the city of Paris, for there I knew there would be given more frequent chance for my assaults in our battle of disputation.

No long time thereafter I was smitten with a grievous illness, brought upon me by my immoderate zeal for study. This illness forced me to turn homeward to my native province, and thus for some years I was as if cut off from France. And yet, for that very reason, I was sought out all the more eagerly by those whose hearts were troubled by the lore of dialectics. But after a few years had passed, and I was whole again from my sickness, I learned that my teacher, that same William Archdeacon of Paris, had changed his former garb and joined an order of the regular clergy. This he had done, or so men said, in order that he might be deemed more deeply religious, and so might be elevated to a loftier rank in the prelacy, a thing which, in truth, very soon came to pass, for he was made bishop of Châlons. Nevertheless, the garb he had donned by reason of his conversion did nought to keep him away either from the city of Paris or from his wonted study of philosophy; and in the very monastery wherein he had shut himself up for the sake of religion he straightway set to teaching again after the same fashion as before.

To him did I return, for I was eager to learn more of rhetoric from his lips; and in the course of our many arguments on various matters, I compelled him by most potent reasoning first to alter his former opinion on the subject of the universals, and finally to abandon it altogether. Now, the basis of this old concept of his regarding the reality of universal ideas was that the same quality formed the essence alike of the abstract whole and of the individuals which were its parts: in other words, that there could be no essential differences among these individuals, all being alike save for such variety as might grow out of the many accidents of existence. Thereafter, however, he corrected this opinion, no longer maintaining that the same quality was the essence of all things, but that, rather, it manifested itself in them through diverse ways. This problem of universals is ever the most vexed one among logicians, to such a degree, indeed, that even Porphyry, writing in his "Isagoge" regarding universals, dared not attempt a final pronouncement thereon, saying rather: "This is the deepest of all problems of its kind." Wherefore it followed that when William had first revised and then finally abandoned altogether his views on this one subject, his lecturing sank into such a state of negligent reasoning that it could scarce be called lecturing on the science of dialectics at all; it was as if all his science had been bound up in this one question of the nature of universals.

Thus it came about that my teaching won such strength and authority that even those who before had clung most vehemently to my former master, and most bitterly attacked my doctrines, now flocked to my school. The very man who had succeeded to my master's chair in the Paris school offered me his post, in order that he might put himself under my tutelage along with all the rest, and this in the very place where of old his master and mine had reigned. And when, in so short a time, my master saw me directing the study of dialectics there, it is not easy to find words to tell with what envy he was consumed or with what pain he was tormented. He could not long, in truth, bear the anguish of what he felt to be his wrongs, and shrewdly he attacked me that he might drive me forth. And because there was nought in my conduct whereby he could come at me openly, he tried to steal away the school by launching the vilest calumnies against him who had yielded his post to me, and by putting in his place a certain rival of mine. So then I returned to Melun, and set up my school there as before; and the more openly his envy pursued me, the greater was the authority it conferred upon me. Even so held the poet: "Jealousy aims at the peaks; the winds storm the loftiest summits." (Ovid: "Remedy for Love," I, 369.)

Not long thereafter, when William became aware of the fact that almost all his students were holding grave doubts as to his religion, and were whispering earnestly among themselves about his conversion, deeming that he had by no means abandoned this world, he withdrew himself and his brotherhood, together with his students, to a certain estate far distant from the city. Forthwith I returned from Melun to Paris, hoping for peace from him in the future. But since, as I have said, he had caused my place to be occupied by a rival of mine, I pitched the camp, as it were, of my school outside the city on Mont Ste. Geneviève. Thus I was as one laying siege to him who had taken possession of my post. No sooner had my master heard of this than he brazenly returned post haste to the city, bringing back with him such students as he could, and reinstating his brotherhood in their for mer monastery, much as if he would free his soldiery, whom he had deserted, from my blockade. In truth, though, if it was his purpose to bring them succour, he did nought but hurt them. Before that time my rival had indeed had a certain number of students, of one sort and another, chiefly by reason of his lectures on Priscian, in which he was considered of great authority. After our master had returned, however, he lost nearly all of these followers, and thus was compelled to give up the direction of the school. Not long thereafter, apparently despairing further of worldly fame, he was converted to the monastic life.

Following the return of our master to the city, the combats in disputation which my scholars waged both with him himself and with his pupils, and the successes which fortune gave to us, and above all to me, in these wars, you have long since learned of through your own experience. The boast of Ajax, though I speak it more temperately, I still am bold enough to make:

> *"... if fain you would learn now*
> *How victory crowned the battle, by him was*
> *I never vanquished."*

> — OVID, "METAMORPHOSES,"
> XIII, 89.

But even were I to be silent, the fact proclaims itself, and its outcome reveals the truth regarding it.

While these things were happening, it became needful for me again to repair to my old home, by reason of my dear mother, Lucia, for after the conversion of my father, Berengarius, to the monastic life, she so ordered her affairs as to do likewise. When all this had been completed, I returned to France, above all in order that I might study theology, since now my oft-mentioned teacher, William, was active in the episcopate of Châlons. In this held of learning Anselm of Laon, who was his teacher therein, had for long years enjoyed the greatest renown.

OF HOW HE CAME TO LAON
TO SEEK ANSELM AS TEACHER

S ought out, therefore, this same venerable man, whose fame, in truth, was more the result of long-established custom than of the potency of his own talent or intellect. If any one came to him impelled by doubt on any subject, he went away more doubtful still. He was wonderful, indeed, in the eyes of these who only listened to him, but those who asked him questions perforce held him as nought. He had a miraculous flock of words, but they were contemptible in meaning and quite void of reason. When he kindled a fire, he filled his house with smoke and illumined it not at all. He was a tree which seemed noble to those who gazed upon its leaves from afar, but to those who came nearer and examined it more closely was revealed its barrenness. When, therefore, I had come to this tree that I might pluck the fruit thereof, I discovered that it was indeed the fig tree which Our Lord cursed (Matthew xxi, 19; Mark xi, 13), or that ancient oak to which Lucan likened Pompey, saying:

> *"... he stands, the shade of a name once mighty,*
> *Like to the towering oak in the midst of the fruitful field."*

> — LUCAN, "PHARSALIA," IV, 135.

It was not long before I made this discovery, and stretched myself lazily in the shade of that same tree. I went to his lectures less and less often, a thing which some among his eminent followers took sorely to heart, because they interpreted it as a mark of contempt for so illustrious a teacher. Thenceforth they secretly sought to influence him against me, and by their vile insinuations made me hated of him. It chanced, moreover, that one day, after the exposition of certain texts, we scholars were jesting among ourselves, and one of them, seeking to draw me out, asked me what I thought of the lectures on the Books of Scripture. I, who had as yet studied only the sciences, replied that following such lectures seemed to me most useful in so far as the salvation of the soul was concerned, but that it appeared quite extraordinary to me that educated persons should not be able to understand the sacred books simply by studying them themselves, together with the glosses thereon, and without the aid of any teacher. Most of those who were present mocked at me, and asked whether I myself could do as I had said, or whether I would dare to undertake it. I answered that if they wished, I was ready to try it. Forthwith they cried out and jeered all the more. "Well and good," said they; "we agree to the test. Pick out and give us an exposition of some doubtful passage in the Scriptures, so that we can put this boast of yours to the proof." And they all chose that most obscure prophecy of Ezekiel.

I accepted the challenge, and invited them to attend a lecture on the very next day. Whereupon they undertook to give me good advice, saying that I should by no means make undue haste in so important a matter, but that I ought to devote a much loner space to working out my exposition and offsetting my inexperience by diligent toil. To this I replied indignantly that it was my wont to win success, not by routine, but by ability. I added that I would abandon the test altogether unless they would agree not to put off their attendance at my lecture. In truth at this first lecture of mine only a few were present, for it seemed quite absurd to all of them that I, hitherto so inexperienced in discussing the Scriptures, should attempt the thing so hastily. However, this lecture gave such satisfaction to all those who heard it that they spread its praises abroad with notable enthusiasm, and thus compelled me to continue my interpretation of the sacred text. When word of this was bruited about, those who had stayed away from the first lecture came eagerly, some to the second and more to the third, and all of them were eager to write down the glosses which I had begun on the first day, so as to have them from the very beginning.

OF THE PERSECUTION HE
HAD FROM HIS TEACHER
ANSELM

Now this venerable man of whom I have spoken was acutely smitten with envy, and straightway incited, as I have already mentioned, by the insinuations of sundry persons, began to persecute me for my lecturing on the Scriptures no less bitterly than my former master, William, had done for my work in philosophy. At that time there were in this old man's school two who were considered far to excel all the others: Alberic of Rheims and Lotulphe the Lombard. The better opinion these two held of themselves, the more they were incensed against me. Chiefly at their suggestion, as it afterwards transpired, yonder venerable coward had the impudence to forbid me to carry on any further in his school the work of preparing glosses which I had thus begun. The pretext he alleged was that if by chance in the course of this work I should write anything containing blunders—as was likely enough in view of my lack of training—the thing might be imputed to him. When this came to the ears of his scholars, they were filled with indignation at so undisguised a manifestation of spite, the like of which had never been directed against any one before. The more obvious this rancour became, the more it redounded to my honour, and his persecution did nought save to make me more famous.

OF HOW HE RETURNED TO PARIS AND FINISHED THE GLOSSES WHICH HE HAD BEGUN AT LAON

And so, after a few days, I returned to Paris, and there for several years I peacefully directed the school which formerly had been destined for me, nay, even offered to me, but from which I had been driven out. At the very outset of my work there, I set about completing the glosses on Ezekiel which I had begun at Laon. These proved so satisfactory to all who read them that they came to believe me no less adept in lecturing on theology than I had proved myself to be in the held of philosophy. Thus my school was notably increased in size by reason of my lectures on subjects of both these kinds, and the amount of financial profit as well as glory which it brought me cannot be concealed from you, for the matter was widely talked of. But prosperity always puffs up the foolish, and worldly comfort enervates the soul, rendering it an easy prey to carnal temptations. Thus I, who by this time had come to regard myself as the only philosopher remaining in the whole world, and had ceased to fear any further disturbance of my peace, began to loosen the rein on my desires, although hitherto I had always lived in the utmost continence. And the greater progress I made in my lecturing on philosophy or theology, the more I departed alike from the practice of the philosophers and the spirit of the divines in the uncleanness of my life. For it is well known, methinks, that philosophers, and still more those who

"

have devoted their lives to arousing the love of sacred study, have been strong above all else in the beauty of chastity.

Thus did it come to pass that while I was utterly absorbed in pride and sensuality, divine grace, the cure for both diseases, was forced upon me, even though I, forsooth, would fain have shunned it. First was I punished for my sensuality, and then for my pride. For my sensuality I lost those things whereby I practiced it; for my pride, engendered in me by my knowledge of letters—and it is even as the Apostle said: "Knowledge puffeth itself up" (I Cor. viii, 1)—I knew the humiliation of seeing burned the very book in which I most gloried. And now it is my desire that you should know the stories of these two happenings, understanding them more truly from learning the very facts than from hearing what is spoken of them, and in the order in which they came about. Because I had ever held in abhorrence the foulness of prostitutes, because I had diligently kept myself from all excesses and from association with the women of noble birth who attended the school, because I knew so little of the common talk of ordinary people, perverse and subtly flattering chance gave birth to an occasion for casting me lightly down from the heights of my own exaltation. Nay, in such case not even divine goodness could redeem one who, having been so proud, was brought to such shame, were it not for the blessed gift of grace.

OF HOW, BROUGHT LOW BY
HIS LOVE FOR HÉLOÏSE, HE
WAS WOUNDED IN BODY
AND SOUL

Now there dwelt in that same city of Paris a certain young girl named Héloïse, the niece of a canon who was called Fulbert. Her uncle's love for her was equalled only by his desire that she should have the best education which he could possibly procure for her. Of no mean beauty, she stood out above all by reason of her abundant knowledge of letters. Now this virtue is rare among women, and for that very reason it doubly graced the maiden, and made her the most worthy of renown in the entire kingdom. It was this young girl whom I, after carefully considering all those qualities which are wont to attract lovers, determined to unite with myself in the bonds of love, and indeed the thing seemed to me very easy to be done. So distinguished was my name, and I possessed such advantages of youth and comeliness, that no matter what woman I might favour with my love, I dreaded rejection of none. Then, too, I believed that I could win the maiden's consent all the more easily by reason of her knowledge of letters and her zeal therefor; so, even if we were parted, we might yet be together in thought with the aid of written messages. Perchance, too, we might be able to write more boldly than we could speak, and thus at all times could we live in joyous intimacy.

Thus, utterly aflame with my passion for this maiden, I sought to discover means whereby I might have daily and familiar speech with her, thereby the more easily to win her consent. For this purpose I persuaded the girl's uncle, with the aid of some of his friends, to take me into his household—for he dwelt hard by my school—in return for the payment of a small sum. My pretext for this was that the care of my own household was a serious handicap to my studies, and likewise burdened me with an expense far greater than I could afford. Now, he was a man keen in avarice, and likewise he was most desirous for his niece that her study of letters should ever go forward, so, for these two reasons, I easily won his consent to the fulfillment of my wish, for he was fairly agape for my money, and at the same time believed that his niece would vastly benefit by my teaching. More even than this, by his own earnest entreaties he fell in with my desires beyond anything I had dared to hope, opening the way for my love; for he entrusted her wholly to my guidance, begging me to give her instruction whensoever I might be free from the duties of my school, no matter whether by day or by night, and to punish her sternly if ever I should find her negligent of her tasks. In all this the man's simplicity was nothing short of astounding to me; I should not have been more smitten with wonder if he had entrusted a tender lamb to the care of a ravenous wolf. When he had thus given her into my charge, not alone to be taught but even to be disciplined, what had he done save to give free scope to my desires, and to offer me every opportunity, even if I had not sought it, to bend her to my will with threats and blows if I failed to do so with caresses? There were, however, two things which particularly served to allay any foul suspicion: his own love for his niece, and my former reputation for continence.

Why should I say more: We were united first in the dwelling that sheltered our love, and then in the hearts that burned with it. Under the pretext of study we spent our hours in the happiness of love, and learning held out to us the secret opportunities that our passion craved. Our speech was more of love than of the book which lay open before us; our kisses far outnumbered our reasoned words. Our hands sought less the book than each other's bosoms; love drew our eyes together far more than the lesson drew them to the pages of our text. In order that there might be no suspicion, there were, indeed, sometimes blows, but love gave them, not anger; they were the marks, not of wrath, but of a tenderness surpassing the most fragrant balm in sweetness. What followed? No degree in love's progress was left untried by our passion, and if love itself could imagine any wonder as yet unknown, we discovered it. And our inexperience of such delights made us all the more ardent in our pursuit of them, so that our thirst for one another was still unquenched.

In measure as this passionate rapture absorbed me more and more, I devoted ever less time to philosophy and to the work of the school. Indeed it became loathsome to me to go to the school or to linger there; the labour, moreover, was very burdensome, since my nights were vigils of love and my days of study. My lecturing became utterly careless and lukewarm; I did nothing because of inspiration, but everything merely as a matter of habit. I had become nothing more than a reciter of my former discoveries, and though I still wrote poems, they dealt with love, not with the secrets of philosophy. Of these songs you yourself well know how some have become widely known and have been sung in many lands, chiefly, methinks, by those who delighted in the things of this world. As for the sorrow, the groans, the lamentations of my students when they perceived the preoccupation, nay, rather the chaos, of my mind, it is hard even to imagine them.

A thing so manifest could deceive only a few, no one, methinks, save him whose shame it chiefly bespoke, the girl's uncle, Fulbert. The truth was often enough hinted to him, and by many persons, but he could not believe it, partly, as I have said, by reason of his boundless love for his niece, and partly because of the well-known continence of my previous life. Indeed we do not easily suspect shame in those whom we most cherish, nor can there be the blot of foul suspicion on devoted love. Of this St. Jerome in his epistle to Sabinianus (Epist. 48) says: "We are wont to be the last to know the evils of our own households, and to be ignorant of the sins of our children and our wives, though our neighbours sing them aloud." But no matter how slow a matter may be in disclosing itself, it is sure to come forth at last, nor is it easy to hide from one what is known to all. So, after the lapse of several months, did it happen with us. Oh, how great was the uncle's grief when he learned the truth, and how bitter was the sorrow of the lovers when we were forced to part! With what shame was I overwhelmed, with what contrition smitten because of the blow which had fallen on her I loved, and what a tempest of misery burst over her by reason of my disgrace! Each grieved most, not for himself, but for the other. Each sought to allay, not his own sufferings, but those of the one he loved. The very sundering of our bodies served but to link our souls closer together; the plentitude of the love which was denied to us inflamed us more than ever. Once the first wildness of shame had passed, it left us more shameless than before, and as shame died within us the cause of it seemed to us ever more desirable. And so it chanced with us as, in the stories that the poets tell, it once happened with Mars and Venus when they were caught together.

It was not long after this that Héloïse found that she was pregnant, and of this she wrote to me in the utmost exultation, at the same time asking me to consider what had best be done. Accordingly, on a night when her uncle was absent, we carried out the plan we had determined on, and I stole her secretly away from her uncle's house, sending her without delay to my own country. She remained there with my sister until she gave birth to a son, whom she named Astrolabe. Meanwhile her uncle, after his return, was almost mad with grief; only one who had then seen him could rightly guess the burning agony of his sorrow and the bitterness of his shame. What steps to take against me, or what snares to set for me, he did not know. If he should kill me or do me some bodily hurt, he feared greatly lest his dear-loved niece should be made to suffer for it among my kinsfolk. He had no power to seize me and imprison me somewhere against my will, though I make no doubt he would have done so quickly enough had he been able or dared, for I had taken measures to guard against any such attempt.

At length, however, in pity for his boundless grief, and bitterly blaming myself for the suffering which my love had brought upon him through the baseness of the deception I had practiced, I went to him to entreat his forgiveness, promising to make any amends that he himself might decree. I pointed out that what had happened could not seem incredible to any one who had ever felt the power of love, or who remembered how, from the very beginning of the human race, women had cast down even the noblest men to utter ruin. And in order to make amends even beyond his extremest hope, I offered to marry her whom I had seduced, provided only the thing could be kept secret, so that I might suffer no loss of reputation thereby. To this he gladly assented, pledging his own faith and that of his kindred, and sealing with kisses the pact which I had sought of him—and all this that he might the more easily betray me.

OF THE ARGUMENTS OF HÉLOÏSE AGAINST WEDLOCK —OF HOW NONE THE LESS HE MADE HER HIS WIFE

Forthwith I repaired to my own country, and brought back thence my mistress, that I might make her my wife. She, however, most violently disapproved of this, and for two chief reasons: the danger thereof, and the disgrace which it would bring upon me. She swore that her uncle would never be appeased by such satisfaction as this, as, indeed, afterwards proved only too true. She asked how she could ever glory in me if she should make me thus inglorious, and should shame herself along with me. What penalties, she said, would the world rightly demand of her if she should rob it of so shining a light! What curses would follow such a loss to the Church, what tears among the philosophers would result from such a marriage! How unfitting, how lamentable it would be for me, whom nature had made for the whole world, to devote myself to one woman solely, and to subject myself to such humiliation! She vehemently rejected this marriage, which she felt would be in every way ignominious and burdensome to me.

Besides dwelling thus on the disgrace to me, she reminded me of the hardships of married life, to the avoidance of which the Apostle exhorts us, saying: "Art thou loosed from a wife? seek not a wife. But and if thou marry, thou hast not sinned; and if a virgin marry, she hath not sinned. Nevertheless such shall have trouble in the flesh: but I spare you" (I Cor. vii, 27). And again: "But I would have you to be free from cares" (I Cor. vii, 32). But if I would heed neither the counsel of the Apostle nor the exhortations of the saints regarding this heavy yoke of matrimony, she bade me at least consider the advice of the philosophers, and weigh carefully what had been written on this subject either by them or concerning their lives. Even the saints themselves have often and earnestly spoken on this subject for the purpose of warning us. Thus St. Jerome, in his first book against Jovinianus, makes Theophrastus set forth in great detail the intolerable annoyances and the endless disturbances of married life, demonstrating with the most convincing arguments that no wise man should ever have a wife, and concluding his reasons for this philosophic exhortation with these words: "Who among Christians would not be overwhelmed by such arguments as these advanced by Theophrastus?"

Again, in the same work, St. Jerome tells how Cicero, asked by Hircius after his divorce of Terentia whether he would marry the sister of Hircius, replied that he would do no such thing, saying that he could not devote himself to a wife and to philosophy at the same time. Cicero does not, indeed, precisely speak of "devoting himself," but he does add that he did not wish to undertake anything which might rival his study of philosophy in its demands upon him.

Then, turning from the consideration of such hindrances to the study of philosophy, Héloïse bade me observe what were the conditions of honourable wedlock. What possible concord could there be between scholars and domestics, between authors and cradles, between books or tablets and distaffs, between the stylus or the pen and the spindle? What man, intent on his religious or philosophical meditations, can possibly endure the whining of children, the lullabies of the nurse seeking to quiet them, or the noisy confusion of family life? Who can endure the continual untidiness of children? The rich, you may reply, can do this, because they have palaces or houses containing many rooms, and because their wealth takes no thought of expense and protects them from daily worries. But to this the answer is that the condition of philosophers is by no means that of the wealthy, nor can those whose minds are occupied with riches and worldly cares find time for religious or philosophical study. For this reason the renowned philosophers of old utterly despised the world, fleeing from its perils rather than reluctantly giving them up, and denied themselves all its delights in order that they might repose in the embraces of philosophy alone. One of them, and the greatest of all, Seneca, in his advice to Lucilius, says: "Philosophy is not a thing to be studied only in hours of leisure; we must give up everything else to devote ourselves to it, for no amount of time is really sufficient thereto" (Epist. 73).

It matters little, she pointed out, whether one abandons the study of philosophy completely or merely interrupts it, for it can never remain at the point where it was thus interrupted. All other occupations must be resisted; it is vain to seek to adjust life to include them, and they must simply be eliminated. This view is maintained, for example, in the love of God by those among us who are truly called monastics, and in the love of wisdom by all those who have stood out among men as sincere philosophers. For in every race, gentiles or Jews or Christians, there have always been a few who excelled their fellows in faith or in the purity of their lives, and who were set apart from the multitude by their continence or by their abstinence from worldly pleasures.

Among the Jews of old there were the Nazarites, who consecrated themselves to the Lord, some of them the sons of the prophet Elias and others the followers of Eliseus, the monks of whom, on the authority of St. Jerome (Epist. 4 and 13), we read in the Old Testament. More recently there were the three philosophical sects which Josephus defines in his Book of Antiquities (xviii, 2), calling them the Pharisees, the Sadducees and the Essenes. In our times, furthermore, there are the monks who imitate either the communal life of the Apostles or the earlier and solitary life of John. Among the gentiles there are, as has been said, the philosophers. Did they not apply the name of wisdom or philosophy as much to the religion of life as to the pursuit of learning, as we find from the origin of the word itself, and likewise from the testimony of the saints?

There is a passage on this subject in the eighth book of St. Augustine's "City of God," wherein he distinguishes between the various schools of philosophy. "The Italian school," he says, "had as its founder Pythagoras of Samos, who, it is said, originated the very word 'philosophy.' Before his time those who were regarded as conspicuous for the praiseworthiness of their lives were called wise men, but he, on being asked of his profession, replied that he was a philosopher, that is to say a student or a lover of wisdom, because it seemed to him unduly boastful to call himself a wise man." In this passage, therefore, when the phrase "conspicuous for the praiseworthiness of their lives" is used, it is evident that the wise, in other words the philosophers, were so called less because of their erudition than by reason of their virtuous lives. In what sobriety and continence these men lived it is not for me to prove by illustration, lest I should seem to instruct Minerva herself.

Now, she added, if laymen and gentiles, bound by no profession of religion, lived after this fashion, what ought you, a cleric and a canon, to do in order not to prefer base voluptuousness to your sacred duties, to prevent this Charybdis from sucking you down headlong, and to save yourself from being plunged shamelessly and irrevocably into such filth as this? If you care nothing for your privileges as a cleric, at least uphold your dignity as a philosopher. If you scorn the reverence due to God, let regard for your reputation temper your shamelessness. Remember that Socrates was chained to a wife, and by what a filthy accident he himself paid for this blot on philosophy, in order that others thereafter might be made more cautious by his example. Jerome thus mentions this affair, writing about Socrates in his first book against Jovinianus: "Once when he was withstanding a storm of reproaches which Xantippe was hurling at him from an upper story, he was suddenly drenched with foul slops; wiping his head, he said only, 'I knew there would be a shower after all that thunder.'"

Her final argument was that it would be dangerous for me to take her back to Paris, and that it would be far sweeter for her to be called my mistress than to be known as my wife; nay, too, that this would be more honourable for me as well. In such case, she said, love alone would hold me to her, and the strength of the marriage chain would not constrain us. Even if we should by chance be parted from time to time, the joy of our meetings would be all the sweeter by reason of its rarity. But when she found that she could not convince me or dissuade me from my folly by these and like arguments, and because she could not bear to offend me, with grievous sighs and tears she made an end of her resistance, saying: "Then there is no more left but this, that in our doom the sorrow yet to come shall be no less than the love we two have already known." Nor in this, as now the whole world knows, did she lack the spirit of prophecy.

So, after our little son was born, we left him in my sister's care, and secretly returned to Paris. A few days later, in the early morning, having kept our nocturnal vigil of prayer unknown to all in a certain church, we were united there in the benediction of wedlock, her uncle and a few friends of his and mine being present. We departed forthwith stealthily and by separate ways, nor thereafter did we see each other save rarely and in private, thus striving our utmost to conceal what we had done. But her uncle and those of his household, seeking solace for their disgrace, began to divulge the story of our marriage, and thereby to violate the pledge they had given me on this point. Héloïse, on the contrary, denounced her own kin and swore that they were speaking the most absolute lies. Her uncle, aroused to fury thereby, visited her repeatedly with punishments. No sooner had I learned this than I sent her to a convent of nuns at Argenteuil, not far from Paris, where she herself had been brought up and educated as a young girl. I had them make ready for her all the garments of a nun, suitable for the life of a convent, excepting only the veil, and these I bade her put on.

When her uncle and his kinsmen heard of this, they were convinced that now I had completely played them false and had rid myself forever of Héloïse by forcing her to become a nun. Violently incensed, they laid a plot against me, and one night, while I, all unsuspecting, was asleep in a secret room in my lodgings, they broke in with the help of one of my servants, whom they had bribed. There they had vengeance on me with a most cruel and most shameful punishment, such as astounded the whole world, for they cut off those parts of my body with which I had done that which was the cause of their sorrow. This done, straightway they fled, but two of them were captured, and suffered the loss of their eyes and their genital organs. One of these two was the aforesaid servant, who, even while he was still in my service, had been led by his avarice to betray me.

OF THE SUFFERING OF HIS BODY—OF HOW HE BECAME A MONK IN THE MONASTERY OF ST. DENIS AND HÉLOISE A NUN AT ARGENTEUIL

Whn morning came the whole city was assembled before my dwelling. It is difficult, nay, impossible, for words of mine to describe the amazement which bewildered them, the lamentations they uttered, the uproar with which they harassed me, or the grief with which they increased my own suffering. Chiefly the clerics, and above all my scholars, tortured me with their intolerable lamentations and outcries, so that I suffered more intensely from their compassion than from the pain of my wound. In truth I felt the disgrace more than the hurt to my body, and was more afflicted with shame than with pain. My incessant thought was of the renown in which I had so much delighted, now brought low, nay, utterly blotted out, so swiftly by an evil chance. I saw, too, how justly God had punished me in that very part of my body whereby I had sinned. I perceived that there was indeed justice in my betrayal by him whom I had myself already betrayed; and then I thought how eagerly my rivals would seize upon this manifestation of justice, how this disgrace would bring bitter and enduring grief to my kindred and my friends, and how the tale of this amazing outrage would spread to the very ends of the earth.

What path lay open to me thereafter? How could I ever again hold up my head among men, when every finger should be pointed at me in scorn, every tongue speak my blistering shame, and when I should be a monstrous spectacle to all eyes? I was overwhelmed by the remembrance that, according to the dread letter of the law, God holds eunuchs in such abomination that men thus maimed are forbidden to enter a church, even as the unclean and filthy; nay, even beasts in such plight were not acceptable as sacrifices. Thus in Leviticus (xxii, 24) is it said: "Ye shall not offer unto the Lord that which hath its stones bruised, or crushed, or broken, or cut." And in Deuteronomy (xxiii, 1), "He that is wounded in the stones, or hath his privy member cut off, shall not enter into the congregation of the Lord."

I must confess that in my misery it was the overwhelming sense of my disgrace rather than any ardour for conversion to the religious life that drove me to seek the seclusion of the monastic cloister. Héloïse had already, at my bidding, taken the veil and entered a convent. Thus it was that we both put on the sacred garb, I in the abbey of St. Denis, and she in the convent of Argenteuil, of which I have already spoken. She, I remember well, when her fond friends sought vainly to deter her from submitting her fresh youth to the heavy and almost intolerable yoke of monastic life, sobbing and weeping replied in the words of Cornelia:

> "... O husband most noble,
>   Who ne'er shouldst have shared my couch! Has fortune such
>   power
>   To smite so lofty a head? Why then was I wedded
>   Only to bring thee to woe? Receive now my sorrow,
>   The price I so gladly pay."
>
> — LUCAN, "PHARSALIA," VIII, 94.

With these words on her lips did she go forthwith to the altar, and lifted therefrom the veil, which had been blessed by the bishop, and before them all she took the vows of the religious life. For my part, scarcely had I recovered from my wound when clerics sought me in great numbers, endlessly beseeching both my abbot and me myself that now, since I was done with learning for the sake of gain or renown, I should turn to it for the sole love of God. They bade me care diligently for the talent which God had committed to my keeping (Matthew, xxv, 15), since surely He would demand it back from me with interest. It was their plea that, inasmuch as of old I had laboured chiefly in behalf of the rich, I should now devote myself to the teaching of the poor. Therein above all should I perceive how it was the hand of God that had touched me, when I should devote my life to the study of letters in freedom from the snares of the flesh and withdrawn from the tumultuous life of this world. Thus, in truth, should I become a philosopher less of this world than of God.

The abbey, however, to which I had betaken myself was utterly worldly and in its life quite scandalous. The abbot himself was as far below his fellows in his way of living and in the foulness of his reputation as he was above them in priestly rank. This intolerable state of things I often and vehemently denounced, sometimes in private talk and sometimes publicly, but the only result was that I made myself detested of them all. They gladly laid hold of the daily eagerness of my students to hear me as an excuse whereby they might be rid of me; and finally, at the insistent urging of the students themselves, and with the hearty consent of the abbot and the rest of the brotherhood, I departed thence to a certain hut, there to teach in my wonted way. To this place such a throng of students flocked that the neighbourhood could not afford shelter for them, nor the earth sufficient sustenance.

Here, as befitted my profession, I devoted myself chiefly to lectures on theology, but I did not wholly abandon the teaching of the secular arts, to which I was more accustomed, and which was particularly demanded of me. I used the latter, however, as a hook, luring my students by the bait of learning to the study of the true philosophy, even as the Ecclesiastical History tells of Origen, the greatest of all Christian philosophers. Since apparently the Lord had gifted me with no less persuasiveness in expounding the Scriptures than in lecturing on secular subjects, the number of my students in these two courses began to increase greatly, and the attendance at all the other schools was correspondingly diminished. Thus I aroused the envy and hatred of the other teachers. Those who sought to belittle me in every possible way took advantage of my absence to bring two principal charges against me: first, that it was contrary to the monastic profession to be concerned with the study of secular books; and, second, that

I had presumed to teach theology without ever having been taught therein myself. This they did in order that my teaching of every kind might be prohibited, and to this end they continually stirred up bishops, archbishops, abbots and whatever other dignitaries of the Church they could reach.

OF HIS BOOK ON THEOLOGY
AND HIS PERSECUTION AT
THE HANDS OF HIS FELLOW
STUDENTS—OF THE
COUNCIL AGAINST HIM

It so happened that at the outset I devoted myself to analyzing the basis of our faith through illustrations based on human understanding, and I wrote for my students a certain tract on the unity and trinity of God. This I did because they were always seeking for rational and philosophical explanations, asking rather for reasons they could understand than for mere words, saying that it was futile to utter words which the intellect could not possibly follow, that nothing could be believed unless it could first be understood, and that it was absurd for any one to preach to others a thing which neither he himself nor those whom he sought to teach could comprehend. Our Lord Himself maintained this same thing when He said: "They are blind leaders of the blind" (Matthew, xv, 14).

Now, a great many people saw and read this tract, and it became exceedingly popular, its clearness appealing particularly to all who sought information on this subject. And since the questions involved are generally considered the most difficult of all, their complexity is taken as the measure of the subtlety of him who succeeds in answering them. As a result, my rivals became furiously angry, and summoned a council to take action against me, the chief instigators therein being my two intriguing enemies of former days, Alberic and Lotulphe. These two, now that both William and Anselm, our erstwhile teachers, were dead, were greedy to reign in their stead, and, so to speak, to succeed them as heirs. While they were directing the school at Rheims, they managed by repeated hints to stir up their archbishop, Rodolphe, against me, for the purpose of holding a meeting, or rather an ecclesiastical council, at Soissons, provided they could secure the approval of Conon, Bishop of Praeneste, at that time papal legate in France. Their plan was to summon me to be present at this council, bringing with me the famous book I had written regarding the Trinity. In all this, indeed, they were successful, and the thing happened according to their wishes.

Before I reached Soissons, however, these two rivals of mine so foully slandered me with both the clergy and the public that on the day of my arrival the people came near to stoning me and the few students of mine who had accompanied me thither. The cause of their anger was that they had been led to believe that I had preached and written to prove the existence of three gods. No sooner had I reached the city, therefore, than I went forthwith to the legate; to him I submitted my book for examination and judgment, declaring that if I had written anything repugnant to the Catholic faith, I was quite ready to correct it or otherwise to make satisfactory amends. The legate directed me to refer my book to the archbishop and to those same two rivals of mine, to the end that my accusers might also be my judges. So in my case was fulfilled the saying: "Even our enemies are our judges" (Deut. Xxxii, 31).

These three, then, took my book and pawed it over and examined it minutely, but could find nothing therein which they dared to use as the basis for a public accusation against me. Accordingly they put off the condemnation of the book until the close of the council, despite their eagerness to bring it about. For my part, everyday before the council convened I publicly discussed the Catholic faith in the light of what I had written, and all who heard me were enthusiastic in their approval alike of the frankness and the logic of my words. When the public and the clergy had thus learned something of the real character of my teaching, they began to say to one another: "Behold, now he speaks openly, and no one brings any charge against him. And this council, summoned, as we have heard, chiefly to take action upon his case, is drawing toward its end. Did the judges realize that the error might be theirs rather than his?"

As a result of all this, my rivals grew more angry day by day. On one occasion Alberic, accompanied by some of his students, came to me for the purpose of intimidating me, and, after a few bland words, said that he was amazed at something he had found in my book, to the effect that, although God had begotten God, I denied that God had begotten Himself, since there was only one God. I answered unhesitatingly: "I can give you an explanation of this if you wish it." "Nay," he replied, "I care nothing for human explanation or reasoning in such matters, but only for the words of authority." "Very well." I said; "turn the pages of my book and you will find the authority likewise." The book was at hand, for he had brought it with him. I turned to the passage I had in mind, which he had either not discovered or else passed over as containing nothing injurious to me. And it was God's will that I quickly found what I sought. This was the following sentence, under the heading "Augustine, On the Trinity, Book I": "Whosoever believes that it is within the power of God to beget Himself is sorely in error; this power is not in God, neither is it in any created thing, spiritual or corporeal. For there is nothing that can give birth to itself."

When those of his followers who were present heard this, they were amazed and much embarrassed. He himself, in order to keep his countenance, said: "Certainly, I understand all that." Then I added: "What I have to say further on this subject is by no means new, but apparently it has nothing to do with the case at issue, since you have asked for the word of authority only, and not for explanations. If, however, you care to consider logical explanations, I am prepared to demonstrate that, according to Augustine's statement, you have yourself fallen into a heresy in believing that a father can possibly be his own son." When Alberic heard this he was almost beside himself with rage, and straightway resorted to threats, asserting that neither my explanations nor my citations of authority would avail me aught in this case. With this he left me.

On the last day of the council, before the session convened, the legate and the archbishop deliberated with my rivals and sundry others as to what should be done about me and my book, this being the chief reason for their having come together. And since they had discovered nothing either in my speech or in what I had hitherto written which would give them a case against me, they were all reduced to silence, or at the most to maligning me in whispers. Then Geoffroi, Bishop of Chartres, who excelled the other bishops alike in the sincerity of his religion and in the importance of his see, spoke thus:

"You know, my lords, all who are gathered here, the doctrine of this man, what it is, and his ability, which has brought him many followers in every field to which he has devoted himself. You know how greatly he has lessened the renown of other teachers, both his masters and our own, and how he has spread as it were the offshoots of his vine from sea to sea. Now, if you impose a lightly considered judgment on him, as I cannot believe you will, you well know that even if mayhap you are in the right there are many who will be angered thereby, and that he will have no lack of defenders. Remember above all that we have found nothing in this book of his that lies before us whereon any open accusation can be based. Indeed it is true, as Jerome says: 'Fortitude openly displayed always creates rivals, and the lightning strikes the highest peaks.' Have a care, then, lest by violent action you only increase his fame, and lest we do more hurt to ourselves through envy than to him through justice. A false report, as that same wise man reminds us, is easily crushed, and a man's later life gives testimony as to his earlier deeds. If, then, you are disposed to take canonical action against him, his doctrine or his writings must be brought forward as evidence, and he must have free opportunity to answer his questioners. In that case, if he is found guilty or if he confesses his error, his lips can be wholly sealed. Consider the words of the blessed Nicodemus, who, desiring to free Our Lord Himself, said: 'Doth our law judge any man before it hear him and know what he doeth?'" (John, vii, 51).

When my rivals heard this they cried out in protest, saying: "This is wise counsel, forsooth, that we should strive against the wordiness of this man, whose arguments, or rather, sophistries, the whole world cannot resist!" And yet, methinks, it was far more difficult to strive against Christ Himself, for Whom, nevertheless, Nicodemus demanded a hearing in accordance with the dictates of the law. When the bishop could not win their assent to his proposals, he tried in another way to curb their hatred, saying that for the discussion of such an important case the few who were present were not enough, and that this matter required a more thorough examination. His further suggestion was that my abbot, who was there present, should take me back with him to our abbey, in other words to the monastery of St. Denis, and that there a large convocation of learned men should determine, on the basis of a careful investigation, what ought to be done. To this last proposal the legate consented, as did all the others.

Then the legate arose to celebrate mass before entering the council, and through the bishop sent me the permission which had been determined on, authorizing me to return to my monastery and there await such action as might be finally taken. But my rivals, perceiving that they would accomplish nothing if the trial were to be held outside of their own diocese, and in a place where they could have little influence on the verdict, and in truth having small wish that justice should be done, persuaded the archbishop that it would be a grave insult to him to transfer this case to another court, and that it would be dangerous for him if by chance I should thus be acquitted. They likewise went to the legate, and succeeded in so changing his opinion that finally they induced him to frame a new sentence, whereby he agreed to condemn my book without any further inquiry, to burn it forthwith in the sight of all, and to confine me for a year in another monastery. The argument they used was that it sufficed for the condemnation of my book that I had presumed to read it in public without the approval either of the Roman pontiff or of the Church, and that, furthermore, I had given it to many to be transcribed. Methinks it would be a notable blessing to the Christian faith if there were more who displayed a like presumption. The legate, however, being less skilled in law than he should have been, relied chiefly on the advice of the archbishop, and he, in turn, on that of my rivals. When the Bishop of Chartres got wind of this, he reported the whole conspiracy to me, and strongly urged me to endure meekly the manifest violence of their enmity. He bade me not to doubt that this violence would in the end react upon them and prove a blessing to me, and counseled me to have no fear of the confinement in a monastery, knowing that within a few days the legate himself, who was now acting under compulsion, would after his departure set me free. And thus he consoled me as best he might, mingling his tears with mine.

OF THE BURNING OF HIS BOOK—OF THE PERSECUTION HE HAD AT THE HANDS OF HIS ABBOT AND THE BRETHREN

Straightway upon my summons I went to the council, and there, without further examination or debate, did they compel me with my own hand to cast that memorable book of mine into the flames. Although my enemies appeared to have nothing to say while the book was burning, one of them muttered something about having seen it written therein that God the Father was alone omnipotent. This reached the ears of the legate, who replied in astonishment that he could not believe that even a child would make so absurd a blunder. "Our common faith," he said, "holds and sets forth that the Three are alike omnipotent." A certain Tirric, a schoolmaster, hearing this, sarcastically added the Athanasian phrase, "And yet there are not three omnipotent Persons, but only One."

This man's bishop forthwith began to censure him, bidding him desist from such treasonable talk, but he boldly stood his ground, and said, as if quoting the words of Daniel: "'Are ye such fools, ye sons of Israel, that without examination or knowledge of the truth ye have condemned a daughter of Israel? Return again to the place of judgment,' (Daniel, xiii, 48—The History of Susanna) and there give judgment on the judge himself. You have set up this judge, forsooth, for the instruction of faith and the correction of error, and yet, when he ought to give judgment, he condemns himself out of his own mouth. Set free today, with the help of God's mercy, one who is manifestly innocent, even as Susanna was freed of old from her false accusers."

Thereupon the archbishop arose and confirmed the legate's statement, but changed the wording thereof, as indeed was most fitting. "It is God's truth," he said, "that the Father is omnipotent, the Son is omnipotent, the Holy Spirit is omnipotent. And whosoever dissents from this is openly in error, and must not be listened to. Nevertheless, if it be your pleasure, it would be well that this our brother should publicly state before us all the faith that is in him, to the end that, according to its deserts, it may either be approved or else condemned and corrected."

When, however, I fain would have arisen to profess and set forth my faith, in order that I might express in my own words that which was in my heart, my enemies declared that it was not needful for me to do more than recite the Athanasian Symbol, a thing which any boy might do as well as I. And lest I should allege ignorance, pretending that I did not know the words by heart, they had a copy of it set before me to read. And read it I did as best I could for my groans and sighs and tears. Thereupon, as if I had been a convicted criminal, I was handed over to the Abbot of St. Médard, who was there present, and led to his monastery as to a prison. And with this the council was immediately dissolved.

The abbot and the monks of the aforesaid monastery, thinking that I would remain long with them, received me with great exultation, and diligently sought to console me, but all in vain. O God, who dost judge justice itself, in what venom of the spirit, in what bitterness of mind, did I blame even Thee for my shame, accusing Thee in my madness! Full often did I repeat the lament of St. Anthony: "Kindly Jesus, where wert Thou?" The sorrow that tortured me, the shame that overwhelmed me, the desperation that wracked my mind, all these I could then feel, but even now I can find no words to express them. Comparing these new sufferings of my soul with those I had formerly endured in my body, it seemed that I was in very truth the most miserable among men. Indeed that earlier betrayal had become a little thing in comparison with this later evil, and I lamented the hurt to my fair name far more than the one to my body. The latter, indeed, I had brought upon myself through my own wrongdoing, but this other violence had come upon me solely by reason of the honesty of my purpose and my love of our faith, which had compelled me to write that which I believed.

The very cruelty and heartlessness of my punishment, however, made every one who heard the story vehement in censuring it, so that those who had a hand therein were soon eager to disclaim all responsibility, shouldering the blame on others. Nay, matters came to such a pass that even my rivals denied that they had had anything to do with the matter, and as for the legate, he publicly denounced the malice with which the French had acted. Swayed by repentance for his injustice, and feeling that he had yielded enough to satisfy their rancour, he shortly freed me from the monastery whither I had been taken, and sent me back to my own. Here, however, I found almost as many enemies as I had in the former days of which I have already spoken, for the vileness and shamelessness of their way of living made them realize that they would again have to endure my censure.

After a few months had passed, chance gave them an opportunity by which they sought to destroy me. It happened that one day, in the course of my reading, I came upon a certain passage of Bede, in his commentary on the Acts of the Apostles, wherein he asserts that Dionysius the Areopagite was the bishop, not of Athens, but of Corinth. Now, this was directly counter to the belief of the monks, who were wont to boast that their Dionysius, or Denis, was not only the Areopagite but was likewise proved by his acts to have been the Bishop of Athens. Having thus found this testimony of Bede's in contradiction of our own tradition, I showed it somewhat jestingly to sundry of the monks who chanced to be near. Wrathfully they declared that Bede was no better than a liar, and that they had a far more trustworthy authority in the person of Hilduin, a former abbot of theirs, who had travelled for a long time throughout Greece for the purpose of investigating this very question. He, they insisted, had by his writings removed all possible doubt on the subject, and had securely established the truth of the traditional belief.

One of the monks went so far as to ask me brazenly which of the two, Bede or Hilduin, I considered the better authority on this point. I replied that the authority of Bede, whose writings are held in high esteem by the whole Latin Church, appeared to me the better. Thereupon in a great rage they began to cry out that at last I had openly proved the hatred I had always felt for our monastery, and that I was seeking to disgrace it in the eyes of the whole kingdom, robbing it of the honour in which it had particularly gloried, by thus denying that the Areopagite was their patron saint. To this I answered that I had never denied the fact, and that I did not much care whether their patron was the Areopagite or some one else, provided only he had received his crown from God. Thereupon they ran to the abbot and told him of the misdemeanour with which they charged me.

The abbot listened to their story with delight, rejoicing at having found a chance to crush me, for the greater vileness of his life made him fear me more even than the rest did. Accordingly he summoned his council, and when the brethren had assembled he violently threatened me, declaring that he would straightway send me to the king, by him to be punished for having thus sullied his crown and the glory of his royalty. And until he should hand me over to the king, he ordered that I should be closely guarded. In vain did I offer to submit to the customary discipline if I had in any way been guilty. Then, horrified at their wickedness, which seemed to crown the ill fortune I had so long endured, and in utter despair at the apparent conspiracy of the whole world against me, I fled secretly from the monastery by night, helped thereto by some of the monks who took pity on me, and likewise aided by some of my scholars.

I made my way to a region where I had formerly dwelt, hard by the lands of Count Theobald (of Champagne). He himself had some slight acquaintance with me, and had compassion on me by reason of my persecutions, of which the story had reached him. I found a home there within the walls of Provins, in a priory of the monks of Troyes, the prior of which had in former days known me well and shown me much love. In his joy at my coming he cared for me with all diligence. It chanced, however, that one day my abbot came to Provins to see the count on certain matters of business. As soon as I had learned of this, I went to the count, the prior accompanying me, and besought him to intercede in my behalf with the abbot. I asked no more than that the abbot should absolve me of the charge against me, and give me permission to live the monastic life wheresoever I could find a suitable place. The abbot, however, and those who were with him took the matter under advisement, saying that they would give the count an answer the day before they departed. It appeared from their words that they thought I wished to go to some other abbey, a thing which they regarded as an immense disgrace to their own. They had, indeed, taken particular pride in the fact that, upon my conversion, I had come to them, as if scorning all other abbeys, and accordingly they considered that it would bring great shame upon them if I should now desert their abbey and seek another. For this reason they refused to listen either to my own plea or to that of the count. Furthermore, they threatened me with excommunication unless I should instantly return; likewise they forbade the prior with whom I had taken refuge to keep me longer, under pain of sharing my excommunication. When we heard this both the prior and I were stricken with fear. The abbot went away still obdurate, but a few days thereafter he died.

As soon as his successor had been named, I went to him, accompanied by the Bishop of Meaux, to try if I might win from him the permission I had vainly sought of his predecessor. At first he would not give his assent, but finally, through the intervention of certain friends of mine, I secured the right to appeal to the king and his council, and in this way I at last obtained what I sought. The royal seneschal, Stephen, having summoned the abbot and his subordinates that they might state their case, asked them why they wanted to keep me against my will. He pointed out that this might easily bring them into evil repute, and certainly could do them no good, seeing that their way of living was utterly incompatible with mine. I knew it to be the opinion of the royal council that the irregularities in the conduct of this abbey would tend to bring it more and more under the control of the king, making it increasingly useful and likewise profitable to him, and for this reason I had good hope of easily winning the support of the king and those about him.

Thus, indeed, did it come to pass. But in order that the monastery might not be shorn of any of the glory which it had enjoyed by reason of my sojourn there, they granted me permission to betake myself to any solitary place I might choose, provided only I did not put myself under the rule of any other abbey. This was agreed upon and confirmed on both sides in the presence of the king and his councellors. Forthwith I sought out a lonely spot known to me of old in the region of Troyes, and there, on a bit of land which had been given to me, and with the approval of the bishop of the district, I built with reeds and stalks my first oratory in the name of the Holy Trinity. And there concealed, with but one comrade, a certain cleric, I was able to sing over and over again to the Lord: "Lo, then would I wander far off, and remain in the wilderness" (Ps. IV, 7).

OF HIS TEACHING IN THE WILDERNESS

No sooner had scholars learned of my retreat than they began to flock thither from all sides, leaving their towns and castles to dwell in the wilderness. In place of their spacious houses they built themselves huts; instead of dainty fare they lived on the herbs of the field and coarse bread; their soft beds they exchanged for heaps of straw and rushes, and their tables were piles of turf. In very truth you may well believe that they were like those philosophers of old of whom Jerome tells us in his second book against Jovinianus.

"Through the senses," says Jerome, "as through so many windows, do vices win entrance to the soul. The metropolis and citadel of the mind cannot be taken unless the army of the foe has first rushed in through the gates. If any one delights in the games of the circus, in the contests of athletes, in the versatility of actors, in the beauty of women, in the glitter of gems and raiment, or in aught else like to these, then the freedom of his soul is made captive through the windows of his eyes, and thus is fulfilled the prophecy: `For death is come up into our windows' (Jer. ix, 21). And then, when the wedges of doubt have, as it were, been driven into the citadels of our minds through these gateways, where will be its liberty? where its fortitude? where its thought of God? Most of all does the sense of touch paint for itself the pictures of past raptures, compelling the soul to dwell fondly upon remembered iniquities, and so to practice in imagination those things which reality denies to it.

"Heeding such counsel, therefore, many among the philosophers forsook the thronging ways of the cities and the pleasant gardens of the countryside, with their well-watered fields, their shady trees, the song of birds, the mirror of the fountain, the murmur of the stream, the many charms for eye and ear, fearing lest their souls should grow soft amid luxury and abundance of riches, and lest their virtue should thereby be defiled. For it is perilous to turn your eyes often to those things whereby you may some day be made captive, or to attempt the possession of that which it would go hard with you to do without. Thus the Pythagoreans shunned all companionship of this kind, and were wont to dwell in solitary and desert places. Nay, Plato himself, although he was a rich man, let Diogenes trample on his couch with muddy feet, and in order that he might devote himself to philosophy established his academy in a place remote from the city, and not only uninhabited but unhealthy as well. This he did in order that the onslaughts of lust might be broken by the fear and constant presence of disease, and that his followers might find no pleasure save in the things they learned."

Such a life, likewise, the sons of the prophets who were the followers of Eliseus are reported to have led. Of these Jerome also tells us, writing thus to the monk Rusticus as if describing the monks of those ancient days: "The sons of the prophets, the monks of whom we read in the Old Testament, built for themselves huts by the waters of the Jordan, and forsaking the throngs and the cities, lived on pottage and the herbs of the field" (Epist. iv).

Even so did my followers build their huts above the waters of the Arduzon, so that they seemed hermits rather than scholars. And as their number grew ever greater, the hardships which they gladly endured for the sake of my teaching seemed to my rivals to reflect new glory on me, and to cast new shame on themselves. Nor was it strange that they, who had done their utmost to hurt me, should grieve to see how all things worked together for my good, even though I was now, in the words of Jerome, afar from cities and the market place, from controversies and the crowded ways of men. And so, as Quintilian says, did envy seek me out even in my hiding place. Secretly my rivals complained and lamented one to another, saying: "Behold now, the whole world runs after him, and our persecution of him has done nought save to increase his glory. We strove to extinguish his fame, and we have but given it new brightness. Lo, in the cities scholars have at hand everything they may need, and yet, spurning the pleasures of the town, they seek out the barrenness of the desert, and of their own free will they accept wretchedness."

The thing which at that time chiefly led me to undertake the direction of a school was my intolerable poverty, for I had not strength enough to dig, and shame kept me from begging. And so, resorting once more to the art with which I was so familiar, I was compelled to substitute the service of the tongue for the labour of my hands. The students willingly provided me with whatsoever I needed in the way of food and clothing, and likewise took charge of the cultivation of the fields and paid for the erection of buildings, in order that material cares might not keep me from my studies. Since my oratory was no longer large enough to hold even a small part of their number, they found it necessary to increase its size, and in so doing they greatly improved it, building it of stone and wood. Although this oratory had been founded in honour of the Holy Trinity, and afterwards dedicated thereto, I now named it the Paraclete, mindful of how I had come there a fugitive and in despair, and had breathed into my soul something of the miracle of divine consolation.

Many of those who heard of this were greatly astonished, and some violently assailed my action, declaring that it was not permissible to dedicate a church exclusively to the Holy Spirit rather than to God the Father. They held, according to an ancient tradition, that it must be dedicated either to the Son alone or else to the entire Trinity. The error which led them into this false accusation resulted from their failure to perceive the identity of the Paraclete with the Spirit Paraclete. Even as the whole Trinity, or any Person in the Trinity, may rightly be called God or Helper, so likewise may It be termed the Paraclete, that is to say the Consoler. These are the words of the Apostle: "Blessed be God, even the Father of our Lord Jesus Christ, the Father of mercies, and the God of all comfort; who comforteth us in all our tribulation" (2 Cor. i, 3). And likewise the word of truth says: "And he shall give you another comforter" (Greek "another Paraclete," John, xiv, 16).

Nay, since every church is consecrated equally in the name of the

Father, the Son and the Holy Spirit, without any difference in their possession thereof, why should not the house of God be dedicated to the Father or to the Holy Spirit, even as it is to the Son? Who would presume to erase from above the door the name of him who is the master of the house? And since the Son offered Himself as a sacrifice to the Father, and accordingly in the ceremonies of the mass the prayers are offered particularly to the Father, and the immolation of the Host is made to Him, why should the altar not be held to be chiefly His to whom above all the supplication and sacrifice are made? Is it not called more rightly the altar of Him who receives than of Him who makes the sacrifice? Who would admit that an altar is that of the Holy Cross, or of the Sepulchre, or of St. Michael, or John, or Peter, or of any other saint, unless either he himself was sacrificed there or else special sacrifices and prayers are made there to him? Methinks the altars and temples of certain ones among these saints are not held to be idolatrous even though they are used for special sacrifices and prayers to their patrons.

Some, however, may perchance argue that churches are not built or altars dedicated to the Father because there is no feast which is solemnized especially for Him. But while this reasoning holds good as regards the Trinity itself, it does not apply in the case of the Holy Spirit. For this Spirit, from the day of Its advent, has had Its special feast of the Pentecost, even as the Son has had since His coming upon earth His feast of the Nativity. Even as the Son was sent into this world, so did the Holy Spirit descend upon the disciples, and thus does It claim Its special religious rites. Nay, it seems more fitting to dedicate a temple to It than to either of the other Persons of the Trinity, if we but carefully study the apostolic authority, and consider the workings of this Spirit Itself. To none of the three Persons did the apostle dedicate a special temple save to the Holy Spirit alone. He does not speak of a temple of the Father, or a temple of the Son, as he does of a temple of the Holy Spirit, writing thus in his first epistle to the Corinthians: "But he that is joined unto the Lord is one spirit." (I Cor. vi, 17). And again: "What? know ye not that your body is the temple of the Holy Spirit which is in you, which ye have of God, and ye are not your own?" (ib. 19).

Who is there who does not know that the sacraments of God's blessings pertaining to the Church are particularly ascribed to the operation of divine grace, by which is meant the Holy Spirit? Forsooth we are born again of water and of the Holy Spirit in baptism, and thus from the very beginning is the body made, as it were, a special temple of God. In the successive sacraments, moreover, the seven-fold grace of the Spirit is added, whereby this same temple of God is made beautiful and is consecrated. What wonder is it, then, if to that Person to Whom the apostle assigned a spiritual temple we should dedicate a material one? Or to what Person can a church be more rightly said to belong than to Him to Whom all the blessings which the church administers are particularly ascribed? It was not, however, with the thought of dedicating my oratory to one Person that I first called it the Paraclete, but for the reason I have already told, that in this spot I found consolation. 'None the less, even if I had done it for the reason attributed to me, the departure from the usual custom would have been in no way illogical.

OF THE PERSECUTION
DIRECTED AGAINST HIM BY
SUNDRY NEW ENEMIES OR, AS
IT WERE, APOSTLES

And so I dwelt in this place, my body indeed hidden away, but my fame spreading throughout the whole world, till its echo reverberated mightily-echo, that fancy of the poet's, which has so great a voice, and nought beside. My former rivals, seeing that they themselves were now powerless to do me hurt, stirred up against me certain new apostles in whom the world put great faith. One of these (Norbert of Prémontré) took pride in his position as canon of a regular order; the other (Bernard of Clairvaux) made it his boast that he had revived the true monastic life. These two ran hither and yon preaching and shamelessly slandering me in every way they could, so that in time they succeeded in drawing down on my head the scorn of many among those having authority, among both the clergy and the laity. They spread abroad such sinister reports of my faith as well as of my life that they turned even my best friends against me, and those who still retained something of their former regard for me were fain to disguise it in every possible way by reason of their fear of these two men.

God is my witness that whensoever I learned of the convening of a new assemblage of the clergy, I believed that it was done for the express purpose of my condemnation. Stunned by this fear like one smitten with a thunderbolt, I daily expected to be dragged before their councils or assemblies as a heretic or one guilty of impiety. Though I seem to compare a flea with a lion, or an ant with an elephant, in very truth my rivals persecuted me no less bitterly than the heretics of old hounded St. Athanasius. Often, God knows, I sank so deep in despair that I was ready to leave the world of Christendom and go forth among the heathen, paying them a stipulated tribute in order that I might live quietly a Christian life among the enemies of Christ. It seemed to me that such people might indeed be kindly disposed toward me, particularly as they would doubtless suspect me of being no good Christian, imputing my flight to some crime I had committed, and would therefore believe that I might perhaps be won over to their form of worship.

OF THE ABBEY TO WHICH HE WAS CALLED AND OF THE PERSECUTION HE HAD FROM HIS SONS, THAT IS TO SAY THE MONKS, AND FROM THE LORD OF THE LAND

While I was thus afflicted with so great perturbation of the spirit, and when the only way of escape seemed to be for me to seek refuge with Christ among the enemies of Christ, there came a chance whereby I thought I could for a while avoid the plottings of my enemies. But thereby I fell among Christians and monks who were far more savage than heathens and more evil of life. The thing came about in this wise. There was in lesser Brittany, in the bishopric of Vannes, a certain abbey of St. Gildas at Ruits, then mourning the death of its shepherd. To this abbey the elective choice of the brethren called me, with the approval of the prince of that land, and I easily secured permission to accept the post from my own abbot and brethren. Thus did the hatred of the French drive me westward, even as that of the Romans drove Jerome toward the East. Never, God knows, would I have agreed to this thing had it not been for my longing for any possible means of escape from the sufferings which I had borne so constantly.

The land was barbarous and its speech was unknown to me; as for the monks, their vile and untameable way of life was notorious almost everywhere. The people of the region, too, were uncivilized and lawless. Thus, like one who in terror of the sword that threatens him dashes headlong over a precipice, and to shun one death for a moment rushes to another, I knowingly sought this new danger in order to escape from the former one. And there, amid the dreadful roar of the waves of the sea, where the land's end left me no further refuge in flight, often in my prayers did I repeat over and over again: "From the end of the earth will I cry unto Thee, when my heart is overwhelmed" (Ps. lxi, 2).

No one, methinks, could fail to understand how persistently that undisciplined body of monks, the direction of which I had thus undertaken, tortured my heart day and night, or how constantly I was compelled to think of the danger alike to my body and to my soul. I held it for certain that if I should try to force them to live according to the principles they had themselves professed, I should not survive. And yet, if I did not do this to the utmost of my ability, I saw that my damnation was assured. Moreover, a certain lord who was exceedingly powerful in that region had some time previously brought the abbey under his control, taking advantage of the state of disorder within the monastery to seize all the lands adjacent thereto for his own use, and he ground down the monks with taxes heavier than those which were extorted from the Jews themselves.

The monks pressed me to supply them with their daily necessities, but they held no property in common which I might administer in their behalf, and each one, with such resources as he possessed, supported himself and his concubines, as well as his sons and daughters. They took delight in harassing me on this matter, and they stole and carried off whatsoever they could lay their hands on, to the end that my failure to maintain order might make me either give up trying to enforce discipline or else abandon my post altogether. Since the entire region was equally savage, lawless and disorganized, there was not a single man to whom I could turn for aid, for the habits of all alike were foreign to me. Outside the monastery the lord and his henchmen ceaselessly hounded me, and within its walls the brethren were forever plotting against me, so that it seemed as if the Apostle had had me and none other in mind when he said: "Without were fightings, within were fears" (II Cor. vii, 5).

I considered and lamented the uselessness and the wretchedness of my existence, how fruitless my life now was, both to myself and to others; how of old I had been of some service to the clerics whom I had now abandoned for the sake of these monks, so that I was no longer able to be of use to either; how incapable I had proved myself in everything I had undertaken or attempted, so that above all others I deserved the reproach, "This man began to build, and was not able to finish" (Luke xiv, 30). My despair grew still deeper when I compared the evils I had left behind with those to which I had come, for my former sufferings now seemed to me as nought. Full often did I groan: "Justly has this sorrow come upon me because I deserted the Paraclete, which is to say the Consoler, and thrust myself into sure desolation; seeking to shun threats I fled to certain peril."

The thing which tormented me most was the fact that, having abandoned my oratory, I could make no suitable provision for the celebration there of the divine office, for indeed the extreme poverty of the place would scarcely provide the necessities of one man. But the true Paraclete Himself brought me real consolation in the midst of this sorrow of mine, and made all due provision for His own oratory. For it chanced that in some manner or other, laying claim to it as having legally belonged in earlier days to his monastery, my abbot of St. Denis got possession of the abbey of Argenteuil, of which I have previously spoken, wherein she who was now my sister in Christ rather than my wife, Héloïse, had taken the veil. From this abbey he expelled by force all the nuns who had dwelt there, and of whom my former companion had become the prioress. The exiles being thus dispersed in various places, I perceived that this was an opportunity presented by God himself to me whereby I could make provision anew for my oratory. And so, returning thither, I bade her come to the oratory, together with some others from the same convent who had clung to her.

On their arrival there I made over to them the oratory, together with everything pertaining thereto, and subsequently, through the approval and assistance of the bishop of the district, Pope Innocent II promulgated a decree confirming my gift in perpetuity to them and their successors. And this refuge of divine mercy, which they served so devotedly, soon brought them consolation, even though at first their life there was one of want, and for a time of utter destitution. But the place proved itself a true Paraclete to them, making all those who dwelt round about feel pity and kindliness for the sisterhood. So that, methinks, they prospered more through gifts in a single year than I should have done if I had stayed there a hundred. True it is that the weakness of womankind makes their needs and sufferings appeal strongly to people's feelings, as likewise it makes their virtue all the more pleasing to God and man. And God granted such favour in the eyes of all to her who was now my sister, and who was in authority over the rest, that the bishops loved her as a daughter, the abbots as a sister, and the laity as a mother. All alike marvelled at her religious zeal, her good judgment and the sweetness of her incomparable patience in all things. The less often she allowed herself to be seen, shutting herself up in her cell to devote herself to sacred meditations and prayers, the more eagerly did those who dwelt without demand her presence and the spiritual guidance of her words.

OF THE EVIL REPORT OF HIS INIQUITY

❧

Before long all those who dwelt thereabouts began to censure me roundly, complaining that I paid far less attention to their needs than I might and should have done, and that at least I could do something for them through my preaching. As a result, I returned thither frequently, to be of service to them in whatsoever way I could. Regarding this there was no lack of hateful murmuring, and the thing which sincere charity induced me to do was seized upon by the wickedness of my detractors as the subject of shameless outcry. They declared that I, who of old could scarcely endure to be parted from her I loved, was still swayed by the delights of fleshly lust. Many times I thought of the complaint of St. Jerome in his letter to Asella regarding those women whom he was falsely accused of loving, when he said (Epist. xcix): "I am charged with nothing save the fact of my sex, and this charge is made only because Paula is setting forth to Jerusalem." And again: "Before I became intimate in the household of the saintly Paula, the whole city was loud in my praise, and nearly every one deemed me deserving of the highest honours of priesthood. But I know that my way to the kingdom of Heaven lies through good and evil report alike."

When I pondered over the injury which slander had done to so great a man as this, I was not a little consoled thereby. If my rivals, I told myself, could but find an equal cause for suspicion against me, with what accusations would they persecute me! But how is it possible for such suspicion to continue in my case, seeing that divine mercy has freed me therefrom by depriving me of all power to enact such baseness? How shameless is this latest accusation! In truth that which had happened to me so completely removes all suspicion of this iniquity among all men that those who wish to have their women kept under close guard employ eunuchs for that purpose, even as sacred history tells regarding Esther and the other damsels of King Ahasuerus (Esther ii, 5). We read, too, of that eunuch of great authority under Queen Candace who had charge of all her treasure, him to whose conversion and baptism the apostle Philip was directed by an angel (Acts viii, 27). Such men, in truth, are enabled to have far more importance and intimacy among modest and upright women by the fact that they are free from any suspicion of lust.

The sixth book of the Ecclesiastical History tells us that the greatest of all Christian philosophers, Origen, inflicted a like injury on himself with his own hand, in order that all suspicion of this nature might be completely done away with in his instruction of women in sacred doctrine. In this respect, I thought, God's mercy had been kinder to me than to him, for it was judged that he had acted most rashly and had exposed himself to no slight censure, whereas the thing had been done to me through the crime of another, thus preparing me for a task similar to his own. Moreover, it had been accomplished with much less pain, being so quick and sudden, for I was heavy with sleep when they laid hands on me, and felt scarcely any pain at all.

But alas, I thought, the less I then suffered from the wound, the greater is my punishment now through slander, and I am tormented far more by the loss of my reputation than I was by that of part of my body. For thus is it written: "A good name is rather to be chosen than great riches" (Prov. xxii, 1). And as St. Augustine tells us in a sermon of his on the life and conduct of the clergy, "He is cruel who, trusting in his conscience, neglects his reputation." Again he says: "Let us provide those things that are good, as the apostle bids us (Rom. xii, 17), not alone in the eyes of God, but likewise in the eyes of men. Within himself each one's conscience suffices, but for our own sakes our reputations ought not to be tarnished, but to flourish. Conscience and reputation are different matters: conscience is for yourself, reputation for your neighbour." Methinks the spite of such men as these my enemies would have accused the very Christ Himself, or those belonging to Him, prophets and apostles, or the other holy fathers, if such spite had existed in their time, seeing that they associated in such familiar intercourse with women, and this though they were whole of body. On this point St. Augustine, in his book on the duty of monks, proves that women followed our Lord Jesus Christ and the apostles as inseparable companions, even accompanying them when they preached (Chap. 4). "Faithful women," he says, "who were possessed of worldly wealth went with them, and ministered to them out of their wealth, so that they might lack none of those things which belong to the substance of life." And if any one does not believe that the apostles thus permitted saintly women to go about with them wheresoever they preached the Gospel, let him listen to the Gospel itself, and learn therefrom that in so doing they followed the example of the Lord. For in the Gospel it is written thus: "And it came to pass afterward, that He went throughout every city and village, preaching and showing the glad tidings of the kingdom of God: and the twelve were with Him, and certain women, which had been healed of evil spirits and infirmities, Mary called Magdalene, and Joanna the wife of Chuza, Herod's steward, and Susanna, and many others, which ministered unto Him of their substance" (Luke viii, i-3).

Leo the Ninth, furthermore, in his reply to the letter of Parmenianus concerning monastic zeal, says: "We unequivocally declare that it is not permissible for a bishop, priest, deacon or subdeacon to cast off all responsibility for his own wife on the grounds of religious duty, so that he no longer provides her with food and clothing; albeit he may not have carnal intercourse with her. We read that thus did the holy apostles act, for St. Paul says: 'Have we not power to lead about a sister, a wife, as well as other apostles, and as the brethren of the Lord, and Cephas?' (I Cor. ix, 5). Observe, foolish man, that he does not say: 'have we not power to embrace a sister, a wife,' but he says 'to lead about,' meaning thereby that such women may lawfully be supported by them out of the wages of their preaching, but that there must be no carnal bond between them."

Certainly that Pharisee who spoke within himself of the Lord, saying: "This man, if He were a prophet, would have known who and what manner of woman this is that toucheth Him: for she is a sinner" (Luke vii, 39), might much more reasonably have suspected baseness of the Lord, considering the matter from a purely human standpoint, than my enemies could suspect it of me. One who had seen the mother of Our Lord entrusted to the care of the young man (John xix, 27), or who had beheld the prophets dwelling and sojourning with widows (I Kings xvii, 10), would likewise have had a far more logical ground for suspicion. And what would my calumniators have said if they had but seen Malchus, that captive monk of whom St. Jerome writes, living in the same but with his wife? Doubtless they would have regarded it as criminal in the famous scholar to have highly commended what he thus saw, saying thereof: "There was a certain old man named Malchus, a native of this region, and his wife with him in his hut. Both of them were earnestly religious, and they so often passed the threshold of the church that you might have thought them the Zacharias and Elisabeth of the Gospel, saving only that John was not with them."

Why, finally, do such men refrain from slandering the holy fathers, of whom we frequently read, nay, and have even seen with our own eyes, founding convents for women and making provision for their maintenance, thereby following the example of the seven deacons whom the apostles sent before them to secure food and take care of the women? (Acts vi, 5). For the weaker sex needs the help of the stronger one to such an extent that the apostle proclaimed that the head of the woman is ever the man (I Cor. xi, 3), and in sign thereof he bade her ever wear her head covered (ib. 5). For this reason I marvel greatly at the customs which have crept into monasteries, whereby, even as abbots are placed in charge of the men, abbesses now are given authority over the women, and the women bind themselves in their vows to accept the same rules as the men. Yet in these rules there are many things which cannot possibly be carried out by women, either as superiors or in the lower orders. In many places we may even behold an inversion of the natural order of things, whereby the abbesses and nuns have authority over the clergy, and even over those who are themselves in charge of the people. The more power such women exercise over men, the more easily can they lead them into iniquitous desires, and in this way can lay a very heavy yoke upon their shoulders. It was with such things in mind that the satirist said:

"There is nothing more intolerable than a rich woman."

— JUVENAL, SAT. VI, V, 459

OF THE PERILS OF HIS ABBEY
AND OF THE REASONS FOR
THE WRITING OF THIS HIS
LETTER

Reflecting often upon all these things, I determined to make provision for those sisters and to undertake their care in every way I could. Furthermore, in order that they might have the greater reverence for me, I arranged to watch over them in person. And since now the persecution carried on by my sons was greater and more incessant than that which I formerly suffered at the hands of my brethren, I returned frequently to the nuns, fleeing the rage of the tempest as to a haven of peace. There, indeed, could I draw breath for a little in quiet, and among them my labours were fruitful, as they never were among the monks. All this was of the utmost benefit to me in body and soul, and it was equally essential for them by reason of their weakness.

But now has Satan beset me to such an extent that I no longer know where I may find rest, or even so much as live. I am driven hither and yon, a fugitive and a vagabond, even as the accursed Cain (Gen. iv, 14). I have already said that "without were fightings, within were fears" (II Cor. vii, 5), and these torture me ceaselessly, the fears being indeed without as well as within, and the fightings wheresoever there are fears. Nay, the persecution carried on by my sons rages against me more perilously and continuously than that of my open enemies, for my sons I have always with me, and I am ever exposed to their treacheries. The violence of my enemies I see in the danger to my body if I leave the cloister; but within it I am compelled incessantly to endure the crafty machinations as well as the open violence of those monks who are called my sons, and who are entrusted to me as their abbot, which is to say their father.

Oh, how often have they tried to kill me with poison, even as the monks sought to slay St. Benedict! Methinks the same reason which led the saint to abandon his wicked sons might encourage me to follow the example of so great a father, lest, in thus exposing myself to certain peril, I might be deemed a rash tempter of God rather than a lover of Him, nay, lest it might even be judged that I had thereby taken my own life. When I had safeguarded myself to the best of my ability, so far as my food and drink were concerned, against their daily plottings, they sought to destroy me in the very ceremony of the altar by putting poison in the chalice. One day, when I had gone to Nantes to visit the count, who was then sick, and while I was sojourning awhile in the house of one of my brothers in the flesh, they arranged to poison me, with the connivance of one of my attendants, believing that I would take no precautions to escape such a plot. But divine providence so ordered matters that I had no desire for the food which was set before me; one of the monks whom I had brought with me ate thereof, not knowing that which had been done, and straightway fell dead. As for the attendant who had dared to undertake this crime, he fled in terror alike of his own conscience and of the clear evidence of his guilt.

After this, as their wickedness was manifest to every one, I began openly in every way I could to avoid the danger with which their plots threatened me, even to the extent of leaving the abbey and dwelling with a few others apart in little cells. If the monks knew beforehand that I was going anywhere on a journey, they bribed bandits to waylay me on the road and kill me. And while I was struggling in the midst of these dangers, it chanced one day that the hand of the Lord smote me a heavy blow, for I fell from my horse, breaking a bone in my neck, the injury causing me greater pain and weakness than my former wound.

Using excommunication as my weapon to coerce the untamed rebelliousness of the monks, I forced certain ones among them whom I particularly feared to promise me publicly, pledging their faith or swearing upon the sacrament, that they would thereafter depart from the abbey and no longer trouble me in any way. Shamelessly and openly did they violate the pledges they had given and their sacramental oaths, but finally they were compelled to give this and many other promises under oath, in the presence of the count and the bishops, by the authority of the Pontiff of Rome, Innocent, who sent his own legate for this special purpose. And yet even this did not bring me peace. For when I returned to the abbey after the expulsion of those whom I have just mentioned, and entrusted myself to the remaining brethren, of whom I felt less suspicion, I found them even worse than the others. I barely succeeded in escaping them, with the aid of a certain nobleman of the district, for they were planning, not to poison me indeed, but to cut my throat with a sword. Even to the present time I stand face to face with this danger, fearing the sword which threatens my neck so that I can scarcely draw a free breath between one meal and the next. Even so do we read of him who, reckoning the power and heaped-up wealth of the tyrant Dionysius as a great blessing, beheld the sword secretly hanging by a hair above his head, and so learned what kind of happiness comes as the result of worldly power (Cicer. 5, Tusc.) Thus did I too learn by constant experience, I who had been exalted from the condition of a poor monk to the dignity of an abbot, that my wretchedness increased with my wealth; and I would that the ambition of those who voluntarily seek such power might be curbed by my example.

And now, most dear brother in Christ and comrade closest to me in the intimacy of speech, it should suffice for your sorrows and the hardships you have endured that I have written this story of my own misfortunes, amid which I have toiled almost from the cradle. For so, as I said in the beginning of this letter, shall you come to regard your tribulation as nought, or at any rate as little, in comparison with mine, and so shall you bear it more lightly in measure as you regard it as less. Take comfort ever in the saying of Our Lord, what he foretold for his followers at the hands of the followers of the devil: "If they have persecuted me, they will also persecute you (John xv, 20). If the world hate you, ye know that it hated me before it hated you. If ye were of the world, the world would love his own" (ib. 18-19). And the apostle says: "All that will live godly in Christ Jesus shall suffer persecution" (II Tim. iii, 12). And elsewhere he says: "I do not seek to please men. For if I yet pleased men, I should not be the servant of Christ" (Galat. i, 10). And the Psalmist says: "They who have been pleasing to men have been confounded, for that God hath despised them."

Commenting on this, St. Jerome, whose heir methinks I am in the endurance of foul slander, says in his letter to Nepotanius: "The apostle says: 'If I yet pleased men, I should not be the servant of Christ.' He no longer seeks to please men, and so is made Christ's servant" (Epist. 2). And again, in his letter to Asella regarding those whom he was falsely accused of loving: "I give thanks to my God that I am worthy to be one whom the world hates" (Epist. 99). And to the monk Heliodorus he writes: "You are wrong, brother, you are wrong if you think there is ever a time when the Christian does not suffer persecution. For our adversary goes about as a roaring lion seeking what he may devour, and do you still think of peace? Nay, he lieth in ambush among the rich."

Inspired by those records and examples, we should endure our persecutions all the more steadfastly the more bitterly they harm us. We should not doubt that even if they are not according to our deserts, at least they serve for the purifying of our soul. And since all things are done in accordance with the divine ordering, let every one of true faith console himself amid all his afflictions with the thought that the great goodness of God permits nothing to be done without reason, and brings to a good end whatsoever may seem to happen wrongfully. Wherefore rightly do all men say: "Thy will be done." And great is the consolation to all lovers of God in the word of the Apostle when he says: "We know that all things work together for good to them that love God" (Rom. viii, 28). The wise man of old had this in mind when he said in his Proverbs: "There shall no evil happen to the just" (Prov. xii, 21). By this he clearly shows that whosoever grows wrathful for any reason against his sufferings has therein departed from the way of the just, because he may not doubt that these things have happened to him by divine dispensation. Even such are those who yield to their own rather than to the divine purpose, and with hidden desires resist the spirit which echoes in the words, "Thy will be done," thus placing their own will ahead of the will of God. Farewell.

APPENDIX

PIERRE ABÉLARD

Petrus Abaelardus (or Abailardus) was born in the year 1079 at Palets, a Breton town not far from Nantes. His father, Berengarius, was a nobleman of some local importance; his mother, Lucia, was likewise of noble family. The name "Abaelardus" is said to be a corruption of "Habelardus," which, in turn, was substituted by himself for the nickname "Bajolardus" given to him in his student days. However the name may have arisen, the famous scholar certainly adopted it very early in his career, and it went over into the vernacular as "Abélard" or "Abailard," though with a multiplicity of variations (in Villon's famous poem, for example, it appears as "Esbaillart").

For the main facts of Abélard's life his own writings remain the best authority, but through his frequent contact with many of the foremost figures in the intellectual and clerical life of the early twelfth century it has been possible to check his own account of his career with considerable accuracy. The story told in the "Historia Calamitatum" covers the events of his life from boyhood to about 1132 or 1133,—in other words, up to approximately his fifty-third or fifty-fourth year. That the account he gives of himself is substantially correct cannot be doubted; making all due allowance for the violence of his feelings, which certainly led him to colour many incidents in a manner unfavourable to his enemies, the main facts tally closely with all the external evidence now available.

A very brief summary of the events of the final years of his life will serve to round out the story. The "Historia Calamitatum" was written while Abélard was still abbot of the monastery of St. Gildas, in Brittany. The terrors of his existence there are fully dwelt on in his autobiographical letter, and finally, in 1134 or 1135, he fled, living for a short time in retirement. In 1136, however, we find him once more lecturing, and apparently with much of his former success, on Mont Ste. Genevieve. His old enemies were still on his trail, and most of all Bernard of Clairvaux, to whose fiery adherence to the faith Abélard's rationalism seemed a sheer desecration. The unceasing activities of Bernard and others finally brought Abélard before an ecclesiastical council at Sens in 1140, where he was formally arraigned on charges of heresy. Had Abélard's courage held good, he might have won his case, for Bernard was frankly terrified at the prospect of meeting so formidable a dialectitian, but Abélard, broken in spirit by the prolonged persecution from which he had suffered, contented himself with appealing to the Pope. The indefatigable Bernard at once proceeded to secure a condemnation of Abélard from Rome, whither the accused man set out to plead his case. On the way, however, he collapsed, both physically and in spirit, and remained for a few months at the abbey of Cluny, whence his friends removed him, a dying man, to the priory of St. Marcel, near Châlons-sur-Saône. Here he died on April 21, 1142.

A discussion of Abélard's position among the scholastic philosophers would necessarily go far beyond the proper limits of a mere historical note. He stands out less commandingly as a constructive philosopher than as a master of dialectics. He was, as even his enemies admitted, a brilliant teacher and an unconquerable logician; he was, moreover, a voluminous writer. Works by him which have been preserved include letters, sermons, philosophical and religious treatises, commentaries on the Bible, on Aristotle and on various other books, and a number of poems.

Many of the misfortunes which the "Historia Calamitatum" relates were the direct outcome of Abélard's uncompromising position as a rationalist, and the document is above all interesting for the picture it gives of the man himself, against the background of early twelfth century France. A few dates will help the general reader to connect the life surrounding Abélard with other and more familiar facts. William the Conqueror had entered England thirteen years before Abélard's birth. The boy was eight years old when the Conqueror died near Rouen during his struggle with Philip of France. He was seventeen when the First Crusade began, and twenty when the crusaders captured Jerusalem.

Two of the men who most profoundly influenced the times in which Abélard lived were Hildebrand, famous as Pope Gregory VII, and Louis VI (the Fat), king of France. It was to Hildebrand that the Church owed much of that regeneration of the spirit which gave it such vitality throughout the twelfth century. Hildebrand died, indeed, when Abélard was only six years old, but he left the Church such a force in the affairs of men as it had never been before. As for Louis the Fat, who reigned from 1108 to 1137, it was he who began to lift the royal power in France out of the shadow which the slothfulness and incompetence of his immediate predecessors, Henry I and Philip I, had cast over it. Discerning enough to see that the chief enemies of the crown were the great nobles, and constantly advised by a minister of exceptional wisdom, Suger, abbot of St. Denis, Louis did his utmost to protect the towns and the churches, and to bring that small part of France wherein his power was felt out of the anarchy and chaos of the eleventh century.

It was the France of Louis VI and Sager which formed the background for the great battle between the realists and the nominalists, the battle in which Abélard played no small part. His life was divided between the towns wherein he taught and the Church which alternately welcomed and denounced him. His fellow-disputants have their places in the history of philosophy; the story of Abélard's love for Héloïse has set him apart, so that he has lived for eight centuries less as a fearless thinker and masterly logician than as one of the glowingly romantic figures of the Middle Ages.

"A FRIEND"

It is not known to whom Abélard's letter was addressed, but it may be guessed that the writer intended it to reach the hands of Héloïse. This actually happened, and the first and most famous letter from

Héloise to Abélard was substantially an answer to the "Historia Calamitatum."

WILLIAM OF CHAMPEAUX

William of Champeaux (Gulielmus Campellensis) was born about 1070 at Champeaux, near Melun. He studied under Anselm of Laon and Roscellinus, his training in philosophy thereby being influenced by both realism and nominalism. His own inclination, however, was strongly towards the former, and it was as a determined proponent of realism that he began to teach in the school of the cathedral of Notre Dame, of which he was made canon in 1103. In 1108 he withdrew to the abbey of St. Victor, and subsequently became bishop of Châlons-sur-Marne. He died in 1121. As a teacher his influence was wide; he was a vigorous defender of orthodoxy and a passionate adversary of the heterodox philosophy of his former master, Roscellinus. That he and Abélard disagreed was only natural, but Abélard's statement that he argued William into abandoning the basic principles of his philosophy is certainly untrue.

"THE UNIVERSALS"

It is not within the province of such a note as this to discuss in detail the great controversy between the realists and the nominalists which dominated the philosophical and, to some extent, the religious thought of France during the first half of the twelfth century. In brief, the realists maintained that the idea is a reality distinct from and independent of the individuals constituting it; their motto, *Universalia sunt realia*, was readily capable of extension far beyond the Church, and William of Champeaux himself carried it to the extent of arguing that nothing is real but the universal. The nominalists, on the other hand, argued that "universals" are mere notions of the mind, and that individuals alone are real; their motto was *Universalia sunt nomina*. Thus the central question in the long controversy concerned the reality of abstract or incorporate ideas, and it is to be observed that the realists held views diametrically opposite to those which the word "realism" today implies. In upholding the reality of the idea, they were what would now be called idealists, whereas their opponents, denying the reality of abstractions and insisting on that of the concrete individual or object, were realists in the modern sense.

The peculiar importance of this controversy lay in its effect on the status of the Church. If nominalism should prevail, then the Church would be shorn of much of its authority, for its greatest power lay in the conception of it as an enduring reality outside of and above all the individuals who shared in its work. It is not strange, then, that the ardent realism of William of Champeaux should have been outraged by the nominalistic logic of Abélard. Abélard, indeed, never went to such extreme lengths as the arch-nominalist, Roscellinus, who was duly condemned for heresy by the Council of Soissons in 1092, but he went quite far enough to win for himself the undying enmity of the leading realists, who were followed by the great majority of the clergy.

PORPHYRY

The Introduction ("Isagoge") to the Categories of Aristotle, Written by the Greek scholar and neoplatonist Porphyry in the third century A.D., was translated into Latin by Boétius, and in this form was extensively used throughout the Middle Ages as a compendium of Aristotelian logic. As a philosopher Porphyry was chiefly important as the immediate successor of Plotinus in the neoplatonic school at Rome, but his "Isagoge" had extraordinary weight among the medieval logicians.

PRISCIAN

The *Institutiones grammaticae* of Priscian (Priscianus Caesariensis) formed the standard grammatical and philological textbook of the Middle Ages, its importance being fairly indicated by the fact that today there exist about a thousand manuscript copies of it.

ANSELM

Anselm of Laon was born somewhere about 1040, and is said to have studied under the famous St. Anselm, later archbishop of Canterbury, at the monastery of Bec. About 1070 he began to teach in Paris, where he was notably successful. Subsequently he returned to Laon, where his school of theology and exegetics became the most famous one in Europe. His most important work, an interlinear gloss on the Scriptures, was regarded as authoritative throughout the later Middle Ages. He died in 1117. That he was something of a pedant is probable, but Abélard's picture of him is certainly very far from doing him justice.

ALBERIC OF RHEIMS AND LOTULPHE THE LOMBARD

Of these two not much is known beyond what Abélard himself tells us. ALberic, indeed, won a considerable reputation, and was highly recommended to Pope Honorius II by St. Bernard. In 1139 Alberic seems to have become archbishop of Bourges, dying two years later. Lotulphe the Lombard is referred to by another authority as Leutaldus Novariensis.

ST. JEROME

The enormous scholarship of St. Jerome, born about 340 and dying September 30, 420, made him not only the foremost authority within the Church itself throughout the Middle Ages, but also one of the chief guides to secular scholarship. Abélard repeatedly quotes from him, particularly from his denunciation of the revival of Gnostic here-sies by Jovinianus and from some of his voluminous epistles. He also refers extensively to the charges brought against Jerome by reason of his teaching of women at Rome in the house of Marcella. One of his pupils, Paula, a wealthy widow, followed him on his journey through Palestine, and built three nunneries at Bethlehem, of which she remained the head up to the time of her death in 404.

ST. AUGUSTINE

Regarding the position of St. Augustine (354-430) throughout the Middle Ages, it is here sufficient to quote a few words of Gustav Krüger: "The theological position and influence of Augustine may be said to be unrivalled. No single name has ever exercised such power over the Christian Church, and no one mind ever made so deep an impression on Christian thought. In him scholastics and mystics, popes and opponents of the papal supremacy, have seen their champion. He was the fulcrum on which Luther rested the thoughts by which be sought to lift the past of the Church out of the rut; yet the judgment of Catholics still proclaims the ideals of Augustine as the only sound basis of pbilosopby."

ABBEY OF ST. DENIS

The abbey of St. Denis was founded about 625 by Dagobert, son of Lothair II, at some distance from the basilica which the clergy of Paris had erected in the fifth century over the saint's tomb. Long renowned as the place of burial for most of the kings of France, the abbey of St. Denis had a particular importance in Abélard's day by reason of its close association with the reigning monarch. The abbot to whom Abélard refers so bitterly was Adam of St. Denis, who began his rule of the monastery about 1094. In 1106 this same Adam chose as his secretary one of the inmates of the monastery, Suger, destined shortly to become the most influential man in France through his position as advisor to Louis VI, and also the foremost historian of his time. Adam died in 1123, and his successor, referred to by Abélard in Chapter X, was none other than Suger himself. From 1127 to 1137 Suger devoted most of his time to the reorganization and reform of the monastery of St. Denis. If we are to believe Abélard, such reform was sorely needed, but other contemporary evidence by no means fully sustains Abélard in his condemnation of Adam and his fellow monks.

ORIGEN

The ALexandrian theological writer Origen, who lived from about 185 to 254, was the most distinguished and the most influential of all the theologians of the ancient Church, with the single exception of Augustine. His incredible industry resulted in such a mass of Writings that Jerome himself asked in despair, "Which of us can read all that he has written?" Origen's self-mutilation, referred to by Abélard, was subsequently used by his enemies as an argument for deposing him from his presbyterial status.

ATHANASIUS

Abélard's tract regarding the power of God to create Himself was one of the many distant echoes of the great Arian-Athanasian controversy of the fourth century. St. Athanasius, bishop of Alexandria, well deserved the title conferred on him by the Church as "the father of orthodoxy," and it was by his name that the doctrine of identity of substance ("the Son is of the same substance with the Father") became known. Much of the life of Athanasius was passed amid persecutions at the hands of his enemies, and on several occasions he was driven into exile.

RODOLPHE, ARCHBISHOP OF RHEIMS

Rodolphe, or, as some authorities call him, Rudolph or Radulph, became archbishop of Rheims in 1114, after having served as treasurer of the cathedral. His importance among the French clergy is attested by the many references to him in contemporary documents.

CONON OF PRAENESTE

Conon, bishop of Praeneste, whose real name may have been Conrad, came to France as papal legate on at least two occasions. He represented Paschal II in 1115 at ecclesiastical councils held in Beauvais, Rheims and Châlons; in 1120 he represented Calixtus II at Soissons on the occasion of Abélard's trial.

GEOFFROI OF CHARTRES

Geoffroi, bishop of Chartres, the second of the name to hold that post, was subsequently a warm friend of St. Bernard. Abélard's high estimate of him is fully confirmed by other contemporary authorities.

ABBOT OF ST. MÉDARD

This abbot was probably, though not certainly, Anselm of Soissons, who became a bishop in 1145. The chronology, however, is confusing.

DIONYSIUS THE AREOPAGITE

The confusion regarding the identity of Dionysius the Areopagite persists to this day, at least to the extent that we do not know the real name of the fourth or fifth century writer who, under this pseudonym, exercised so profound an influence on medieval thought. That he was not the bishop of either Athens or Corinth, nor yet the Dionysius who became the patron saint of France, is clear enough. Of the actual Dionysius the Areopagite we know practically nothing. He is mentioned in Acts, xvii, 34, as one of those Athenians who believed when they had heard Paul preach on Mars Hill. A century or more later we learn from another Dionysius, bishop of Corinth, that Dionysius the Areopagite was the first bishop of Athens, a statement of doubtful value. In the fourth or fifth century a Greek theological writer of extraordinary erudition assumed the name of Dionysius the Areopagite, and as his works exerted an enormous influence on later scholarship, it was quite natural that the personal legend of the real Dionysius should have been extended correspondingly.

The Hilduin referred to by Abélard, who was abbot of St. Denis from 814 to 840, was directly responsible for the extreme phase of this extension. Accepting, as most of his contemporaries unquestioningly did, the identity of the theological writer with the Dionysius mentioned in Acts and spoken of as bishop of Athens, Hilduin went one step further, and demonstrated that this Dionysius was likewise the Dionysius (Denis) who had been sent into Gaul and martyred at Catulliacus, the modern St. Denis. There is no evidence to support Hilduin's contention, and the chronology of Gregory of Tours is quite sufficient to disprove it, but none the less it was enthusiastically accepted in France, and above all by the monks of St. Denis.

There was, however, a persistent doubt as to the identity of the Dionysius whose writings had become so famous. Bede, the authority quoted by Abélard, was, of course, wrong in saying that he was the bishop of Corinth, but anything which tended to shake the triple identity, established by Hilduin, of the Dionysius of Athens who listened to St. Paul, of the pseudo-Areopagite whose works were known to every medieval scholar, and of the St. Denis who had become the patron saint of France, was naturally anathematized by the monks who bore the saint's name. Bede and Abélard were by no means accurate, but

Bede's inkling of the truth was quite enough to get Abélard into serious trouble.

THEOBALD OF CHAMPAGNE

Theobald II, Count of Blois, Meaux and Champagne, was one of the most powerful nobles in France, and by the extent of his influence fully deserved the title of "the Great" by which he was subsequently known. His domain included the modern departments of Ardennes, Marne, Aube and Haute-Marne, with part of Aisne, Seine-et-Marne, Yonne and Meuse. Furthermore, his mother Adela, was the daughter of William I of England, and his younger brother, Stephen, was King of England from 1135 to 1154. Theobald became Count of Blois in 1102, Count of Champagne in 1125, and Count of Troyes in 1128. Had he so chosen, he might likewise have become Duke of Normandy after the death of his uncle, Henry I of England, in 1135. He died in 1152.

STEPHEN THE SENESCHAL

There is much doubt as to whether this Stephen was Stephen de Garland, *dapifer*, or another Stephen, who was royal chancellor under Louis the Fat. A charter of the year 1124 is signed by both Stephen *dapifer* and Stephen *cancellarius*. Probably, however, the authority identifying Stephen *dapifer* as Stephen de Garland, seneschal of France, is trustworthy.

THE PARACLETE

Among the terms which are characteristic of, or even peculiar to, the Gospel of St. John is that of "the Paraclete," rendered in the King games version "the Comforter." The Greek word of which "Paraclete" is a reproduction literally means "advocate," one called to aid; hence "intercessor." The doctrine of the Paraclete appears chiefly in John, xiv and xv. For example: (xiv, 16-17) "And I will pray the Father, and he shall give you another Comforter (Paraclete) that be may abide with you for ever; even the spirit of truth." Again: (xiv, 26) "But the Comforter (Paraclete), which is the Holy Ghost, whom the Father will send in my name, he shall teach you all things." With John's words as a basis, the Paraclete came to be regarded as identical with the Third Person of the Trinity, but always with the special attributes of consolation and intercession.

NORBERT OF PRÉMONTRÉ

In 1120 there was established at Prémontré, a desert place in the diocese of Laon, a monastery of canons regular who followed the so-called Rule of St. Augustine, but with supplementary statutes which made the life one of exceptional severity. The head of this monastery was Norbert, subsequently canonized. His order received papal approbation in 1126, and thereafter it spread rapidly throughout Europe; two hundred years later there were no less than seventeen hundred Norbertine or Premonstratensian monasteries. Norbert himself became archbishop of Magdeburg, and it was in Germany that the most notable work of his order was accomplished.

BERNARD OF CLAIRVAUX

Regarding the illustrious St. Bernard, abbot of Clairvaux, it is needless here to say more than that his own age recognized in him the embodiment of the highest ideal of medieval monasticism. Intellectually inferior to Abélard and to some others of those over whom he triumphed, he was their superior in moral strength, in zeal, and above all in the power of making others share his own enthusiasms. Born in 1090, he was renowned as one of the foremost of French churchmen before he was thirty years old; his share in the contest which followed the death of Pope Honorius II in 1130 made him one of the most commanding figures in all Europe. It was to him that the Cistercian order owed its extraordinary expansion in the twelfth century. That Abélard should have fallen before so redoubtable an adversary (see the note on Pierre Abélard) is in no way surprising, but there can be no doubt that St. Bernard's "persecution" of Abélard was inspired solely by high ideals and an intense zeal for the truth as Bernard perceived it.

ABBEY OF ST. GILDAS

Traditionally, at least, this abbey was the oldest one in Brittany.

According to the anonymous author of the Life and Deeds of St. Gildas, it was founded during the reign of Childeric, the second of the Merovingian kings, in the fifth century. Be that as it may, its authentic history had been extensive before Abélard assumed the direction of its affairs. His gruesome picture of the conditions which prevailed there cannot, of course, be accepted as wholly accurate, but even allowing for gross exaggeration, the life of the monks must have been quite sufficiently scandalous. It was apparently in the closing period of Abélard's sojourn at the abbey of St. Gildas that he wrote the "Historia Calamitatum." He endured the life there for nearly ten years; the date of his flight is not certain, but it cannot have been far from 1134 or 1135.

LEO IX

Leo IX, pope from 1049 to 1054, was a native of Upper Alsace. It was at the Easter synod of 1049 that he enjoined anew the celibacy of the clergy, in connection with which the letter quoted by Abélard was written.

LETTERS OF ABELARD
AND HELOISE

PREFACE

It is very surprising that the *Letters of Abelard and Heloise* have not sooner appeared in English, since it is generally allowed, by all who have seen them in other languages, that they are written with the greatest passion of any in this kind which are extant. And it is certain that the *Letters from a Nun to a Cavalier*, which have so long been known and admired among us, are in all respects inferior to them. Whatever those were, these are known to be genuine Pieces occasioned by an amour which had very extraordinary consequences, and made a great noise at the time when it happened, being between two of the most distinguished Persons of that age.

These *Letters*, therefore, being truly written by the Persons themselves, whose names they bear, and who were both remarkable for their genius and learning, as well as by a most extravagant passion for each other, are every where full of sentiments of the heart, (which are not to be imitated in a feigned story,) and touches of Nature, much more moving than any which could flow from the Pen of a Writer of Novels, or enter into the imagination of any who had not felt the like emotions and distresses.

They were originally written in Latin, and are extant in a Collection of the Works of *Abelard*, printed at Paris in the year 1616. With what elegance and beauty of stile they were written in that language, will sufficiently appear to the learned Reader, even by those few citations which are set at the bottom of the page in some places of the following history. But the Book here mentioned consisting chiefly of school-divinity, and the learning of those times, and therefore being rarely to be met with but in public libraries, and in the hands of some learned men, the Letters of *Abelard* and *Heloise* are much more known by a Translation, or rather Paraphrase of them, in French, first published at the Hague in 1693, and which afterwards received several other more complete Editions. This Translation is much applauded, but who was the Author of it is not certainly known. Monsieur Bayle says he had been informed it was done by a woman; and, perhaps, he thought no one besides could have entered so thoroughly into the passion and tenderness of such writings, for which that sex seems to have a more natural disposition than the other. This may be judged of by the Letters themselves, among which those of *Heloise* are the most moving, and the Master seems in this particular to have been excelled by the Scholar.

In some of the later Editions in French, there has been prefixed to the Letters an Historical Account of *Abelard* and *Heloise*; this is chiefly extracted from the Preface of the Editor of *Abelard's* Works in Latin, and from the *Critical Dictionary* of Monsieur Bayle[1], who has put together, under several articles, all the particulars he was able to collect concerning these two famous Persons; and though the first Letter of *Abelard to Philintus*, in which he relates his own story, may seem to have rendered this account in part unnecessary; yet the Reader will not be displeased to see the thread of the relation entire, and continued to the death of the Persons whose misfortunes had made their lives so very remarkable.

It is indeed impossible to be unmoved at the surprising and multiplied afflictions and persecutions which befel a man of *Abelard's* fine genius, when we see them so feelingly described by his own hand. Many of these were owing to the malice of such as were his enemies on the account of his superior learning and merit; yet the great calamities of his life took their rise from his unhappy indulgence of a criminal passion, and giving himself a loose to unwarrantable pleasures. After this he was perpetually involved in sorrow and distress, and in vain sought for ease and quiet in a monastic life. The *Letters* between him and his beloved *Heloise* were not written till long after their marriage and separation, and when each of them was dedicated to a life of religion. Accordingly we find in them surprising mixtures of devotion and tenderness, and remaining frailty, and a lively picture of human nature in its contrarieties of passion and reason, its infirmities, and its sufferings.

---

1. *Vide Artic*. Abelard, Heloise, Foulques, *and* Paraclete

The History of Abelard and Heloise

Peter Abelard was born in the village of Palais in Britany. He lived in the twelfth century, in the reigns of *Louis the Gross*, and *Louis the Young*. His Father's name was *Beranger*, a gentleman of a considerable and wealthy family. He took care to give his children a liberal and pious education, especially his eldest son *Peter*, on whom he endeavoured to bestow all possible improvements, because there appeared in him an extraordinary vivacity of wit joined with sweetness of temper, and all imaginable presages of a great man.

When he had made some advancement in learning, he grew so fond of his books, that, lest affairs of the world might interrupt his proficiency in them, he quitted his birthright to his younger brothers, and applied himself entirely to the studies of Philosophy and Divinity.

Of all the sciences to which he applied himself, that which pleased him most, and in which he made the greatest progress, was Logick. He had a very subtile wit, and was incessantly whetting it by disputes, out of a restless ambition to be master of his weapons. So that in a short time he gained the reputation of the greatest philosopher of his age; and has always been esteemed the founder of what we call the *Learning of the Schoolmen*.

He finished his studies at Paris, where learning was then in a flourishing condition. In this city he found that famous professor of philosophy William des Champeaux, and soon became his favourite scholar;

but this did not last long. The professor was so hard put to it to answer the subtle objections of his new scholar, that he grew uneasy with him. The school soon run into parties. The senior scholars, transported with envy against *Abelard*, seconded their master's resentment. All this served only to increase the young man's presumption, who now thought himself sufficiently qualified to set up a school of his own. For this purpose he chose an advantageous place, which was the town of Melun, ten leagues from Paris, where the French court resided at that time. Champeaux did all that he could to hinder the erecting of this school; but some of the great courtiers being his enemies, the opposition he made to it only promoted the design of his rival.

The reputation of this new professor made a marvellous progress, and eclipsed that of Champeaux. These successes swelled *Abelard* so much that he removed his school to Corbeil, in order to engage his enemy the more closer in more frequent disputations. But his excessive application to study brought upon him a long and dangerous sickness, which constrained him to return to his own native air.

After he had spent two years in his own country he made a second adventure to Paris, where he found that his old antagonist Champeaux had resigned his chair to another, and was retired into a convent of Canons Regular, among whom he continued his lectures. *Abelard* attacked him with such fury, that he quickly forced him to renounce his tenets. Whereupon the poor monk became so despicable, and his antagonist in such great esteem, that nobody went to the lectures of Champeaux, and the very man who succeeded him in his professorship, listed under *Abelard*, and became his scholar.

He was scarce fixed in his chair before he found himself exposed more than ever to the strokes of the most cruel envy. Endeavours were used to do him ill offices by all those who were any ways disaffected to him. Another professor was put into his place, who had thought it his duty to submit to *Abelard*, in short so many enemies were raised against him that he was forced to retreat from Paris to Melun, and there revived his logick lectures. But this held not long; for hearing that Champeaux with all his infantry was retired into a country village, he came and posted himself on mount St. Genevieve, where he erected a new school, like a kind of battery against him whom Champeaux had left to teach at Paris.

Champeaux understanding that his substitute was thus besieged in his school, brought the Regular Canons attack again to their monastery. But this, instead of relieving his friend, caused all his scholars to desert him. At which the poor philosopher was so mortified, that he followed the example of his patron Champeaux, and turned monk too.

The dispute now lay wholly between Abelard and Champeaux, who renewed it with great warmth on both sides; but the senior had not the best on't. While it was depending, *Abelard* was obliged to visit his father and mother, who, according to the fashion of those times, had resolved to forsake the world, and retire into convents, in order to devote themselves more seriously to the care of their salvation.

Having assisted at the admission of his parents into their respective monasteries and received their blessing, he returned to Paris, where during his absence, his rival had been promoted to the bishoprick of Chalons. And now being in a condition to quit his school without any suspicions of flying from his enemy, he resolved to apply himself wholly to Divinity.

To this end he removed to Laon, where one *Anselm* read divinity-lectures with good reputation. But *Abelard* was so little satisfied with the old man's abilities, who has he says, had a very mean genius, and a great fluency of words without sense, that he took a resolution for the future to hear no other master than the Holy Scriptures. A good resolution! if a man takes the Spirit of God for his guide, and be more concerned to distinguish truth from falsehood, than to confirm himself in those principles into which his, own fancy or complexion, or the prejudices of his birth and education, have insensibly led him.

Abelard, together with the Holy Scriptures, read the ancient fathers and doctors of the church, in which he spent whole days and nights, and profited so well, that instead of returning to *Anselm's* lectures, he took up the same employment, and began to explain the Prophet *Ezekiel* to some of his fellow-pupils. He performed this part so agreeably; and in so easy a method that he soon got a crowd of auditors.

The jealous *Anselm* could not bear this; he quickly found means to get the lecturer silenced. Upon this *Abelard* removed to Paris once more, where he proceeded with his public exposition on Ezekiel, and soon acquired the same reputation for his divinity he had before gained for his philosophy. His eloquence and learning procured him an incredible number of scholars from all parts; so that if he had minded saving of money, he might have grown rich with ease in a short time. And happy had it been for him, if, among all the enemies his learning exposed him to, he had guarded his heart against the charms of love. But, alas! the greatest doctors are not always the wisest men, as appears from examples in every age; but from none more remarkable than that of this learned man, whose story I am now going to tell you.

Abelard, besides his uncommon merit as a scholar, had all the accomplishments of a gentleman. He had a greatness of soul which nothing could shock; his passions were delicate, his judgment solid, and his taste exquisite. He was of a graceful person, and carried himself with the air of a man of quality. His conversation was sweet, complaisant, easy, and gentleman-like. It seemed as tho' Nature had designed him for a more elevated employment than that of teaching the sciences. He looked upon riches and grandeur with contempt, and had no higher ambition than to make his name famous among learned men, and to be reputed the greatest doctor of his age: but he had human frailty, and all his philosophy could not guard him from the attacks of love. For some time indeed, he had defended himself against this passion pretty well, when the temptation was but slight; but upon a more intimate familiarity with such agreeable objects, he found his reason fail him: yet in respect to his wisdom, he thought of compounding the matter and resolved at first, that love and philosophy should dwell together in the same breast. He intended only to let out his heart to the former, and that but for a little while; never considering that love is a great ruiner of projects; and that when it has once got a share in a heart, it is easy to possess itself of the whole.

He was now in the seven or eight and twentieth year of his age, when he thought himself completely happy in all respects, excepting that he wanted a mistress. He considered therefore of making a choice, but such a one as might be most suitable to his notions, and the design he had of passing agreeably those hours he did not employ in his study. He had several ladies in his eye, to whom as he says in one of his *Letters*, he could easily have recommended himself. For you must understand, that besides his qualifications mentioned before, he had a vein of poetry, and made abundance of little easy songs, which he would sing with all the advantage of a gallant air and pleasant voice. But tho' he was cut out for a lover, he was not over-hasty in determining his choice. He was not of a humour to be pleased with the wanton or forward; he scorned easy pleasures, and sought to encounter with difficulties and impediments, that he might conquer with the greater glory. In short, he had not yet seen the woman he was to love.

Not far from the place where *Abelard* read his lectures lived one *Doctor Fulbert*, a canon of the church of Notre-Dame. This canon had a niece named *Heloise* in his house whom he educated with great care and affection. Some writers say[1], that she was the good man's natural daughter; but that, to prevent a public scandal, he gave out that she was his niece by his sister, who upon her death-bed had charged him with her education. But though it was well known in those times, as well as since, that the niece of an ecclesiastick is sometimes more nearly related to him, yet of this damsel's birth and parentage we have nothing very certain. There is reason to think, from one of her *Letters to Abelard*, that she came of a mean family; for she owns that great honour was done to her side by this alliance, and that he married much below himself. So that what Francis d'Amboise says, that she was of the name and family of Montmorency has no manner of foundation. It is very probable she was really and truly Fulbert's niece, as he affirmed her to be. Whatever she was for birth, she was a very engaging woman; and if she was not a perfect beauty, she appeared such at least in *Abelard's* eyes. Her person was well proportioned, her features regular, her eyes sparkling, her lips vermillion and well formed, her complexion animated, her air fine, and her aspect sweet and agreeable. She had a surprising quickness of wit, an incredible memory, and a considerable share of learning, joined with humility; and all these accomplishments were attended with something so graceful and moving, that it was impossible for those who kept her company not to be in love with her.

As soon as *Abelard* had seen her, and conversed with her, the charms of her wit and beauty made such an impression upon his heart, that he presently conceived a most violent passion for her, and resolved to make it his whole endeavour to win her affections. And now, he that formerly quitted his patrimony to pursue his studies, laid aside all other engagements to attend his new passion.

In vain did Philosophy and Reason importune him to return; he was deaf to their call, and thought of nothing but how to enjoy the sight and company of his dear *Heloise*. And he soon met with the luckiest opportunity in the world. Fulbert who had the greatest affection imaginable for his niece, finding her to have a good share of natural wit, and a particular genius for learning, thought himself obliged to improve the talents which Nature had so liberally bestowed on her. He had already put her to learn several languages, which she quickly came to understand so well, that her fame began to spread itself abroad, and the wit and learning of *Heloise* was every where discoursed of. And though her uncle for his own share was no great scholar, he was very felicitous that his niece should have all possible improvements. He was willing, therefore, she should have masters to instruct her in what she had a mind to learn: but he loved his money, and this kept him from providing for her education so well as she desired.

Abelard, who knew *Heloise's* inclinations, and the temper of her uncle, thought this an opportunity favourable to his design. He was already well acquainted with Fulbert, as being his brother canon in the same church; and he observed how fond the other was of his friendship, and what an honour he esteemed it to be intimate with a person of his reputation. He therefore told him one day in familiarity, that he was at a loss for some house to board in; and if you could find room for me, said he, in yours, I leave to you name the terms.

The good man immediately considering that by this means he should provide an able master for his niece who, instead of taking money of him, offered to provide him well for his board, embraced his proposal with the joy imaginable, gave him a thousand caresses, and desired he would consider him for the future as one ambitious of the strictest friendship with him.

What an unspeakable joy was this to the amorous *Abelard*! to consider that he was going to live with her, who was the only object of his desires! that he should have the opportunity of seeing and conversing with her every day, and of acquainting her with his passion! However, he concealed his joy at present lest he should make his intention suspected. We told you before how liberal Nature had been to our lover in making his person every way so agreeable; so that he flattered himself that it was almost impossible [2] that any woman should reject his addresses. Perhaps he was mistaken: the sex has variety of humour. However, consider him as a philosopher who had therto lived in a strict chastity [3], he certainly reasoned well in the business of love; when he concluded that *Heloise* would be an easier conquest to him than others because her learning gave him an opportunity of establishing a correspondence by letters, in which he might discover his passion with greater freedom than he dared presume to use in conversation.

Some time after the Canon had taken *Abelard* into his own house, as they were discoursing one day about things somewhat above Fulbert's capacity, the latter turned the discourse insensibly to the good qualities of his niece; he informed *Abelard* of the excellency of her wit, and how strong a propensity she had to improve in learning; and withal made it his earnest request, that he would take the pains to instruct her. *Abelard* pretended to be surprised at a proposal of this nature. He told him that learning was not the proper business of women; that such inclinations in them had more of humour or curiosity than a solid desire of knowledge; and could hardly pass, among either the learned or ignorant, without drawing upon them the imputation of conceit and affectation. Fulbert answered, that this was very true of women of common capacities; but he hoped, when he had discoursed with his niece, and found what progress she had made already, and what a capacity she had for learning, he would be of another opinion. *Abelard* assured him, he was ready to do all he could for her improvement, and if she was not like other women, who hate to learn any thing beyond their needle, he would spare no pains to make *Heloise* answer the hopes which her uncle had conceived of her.

The canon was transported with the civility of the young doctor; he returned him thanks, and protested he could not do him a more acceptable service than to assist his niece in her endeavours to learn; he therefore entreated him once more to set apart some of his time, which he did not employ in public, for this purpose: and, (as if he had known his designed intrigue, and was willing to promote it) he committed her entirely to his care, and begged of him to treat her with the authority of a master; not only to chide her, but even to correct her whenever she was guilty of any neglect or disobedience to his commands.

Fulbert, in this, showed a simplicity without example but the affection which he had for his niece was so blind, and *Abelard* had so well established his reputation for wisdom, that the uncle never scrupled in the least to trust them together, and thought he had all the security in the world for their virtue. *Abelard* you may be sure, made use of the freedom which was given him. He saw his beautiful creature every hour, he set her lessons every day, and was extremely pleased to see what proficiency she made. *Heloise*, for her part, was so taken with her master, that she liked nothing so well as what she learned from him; and the master was charmed with that quickness of apprehension with which his scholar learned the most difficult lessons. But he did not intend to stop here. He knew so well how to insinuate into the affections of this young person, he gave her such plain intimations of what was in his heart and spoke so agreeably of the passion which he had conceived for her, that he had the satisfaction of seeing himself well understood. It is no difficult matter to make a girl of eighteen in love; and *Abelard* having so much wit and agreeable humour, must needs make a greater progress in her affections than she did in the lessons which he taught her; so that in a short time she fell so much in love with him, that she could deny him nothing.

Fulbert had a country-house at Corbeil, to which the lovers often resorted, under pretence of applying themselves more closely to their studies: there they conversed freely and gave themselves up entirely to the pleasure of a mutual passion. They took advantage of that privacy which study and contemplation require without subjecting themselves to the censure of those who observed it.

In this retirement *Abelard* owns that more time was employ'd in soft caresses than in lectures of philosophy. Sometimes he pretended to use the severity of a master; the better to deceive such as might be spies upon them, he exclaimed against *Heloise*, and reproached her for her negligence. But how different were his menaces from those which are inspired by anger!

Never did two lovers give a greater loose to their delights than did these two for five or six months; they lived in all the endearments which could enter into the hearts of young beginners. This is *Abelard's* own account of the matter. He compares himself to such as have been long kept in a starving condition, and at last are brought to a feast. A grave and studious man exceeds a debauchee in his enjoyments of a woman whom he loves and of whom he is passionately beloved.

Abelard being thus enchanted with the caresses of his mistress, neglected all his serious and important affairs. His performances in public were wretched. His scholars perceived it, and soon guessed the reason. His head was turned to nothing but amorous verses. His school was his aversion, and he spent as little time in it as he could. As for his lectures they were commonly the old ones served up again: the night was wholly lost from his studies; and his leisure was employed in writing songs, which were dispersed and sung in diverse provinces of France many years after. In short our lovers, who were in their own opinion the happiest pair in the world, kept so little guard, that their amours were every where talked of, and all the world saw plainly that the sciences were not always the subject of their conversation. Only honest Fulbert, under whose nose all this was done, was the last man that heard any thing of it; he wanted eyes to see that which was visible to all the world; and if any body went about to tell him of it, he was prepossessed with so good an opinion of his niece and her master, that he would believe nothing against them.

But at last so many discoveries were daily made to him, that he could not help believing something; he therefore resolved to separate them, and by that means prevent the ill consequences of their too great familiarity. However, he thought it best to convict them himself, before he proceeded further; and therefore watched them so closely, that he had one day an opportunity of receiving ocular satisfaction that the reports he had heard were true. In short he surprised them together. And though he was naturally cholerick, yet he appeared so moderate on this occasion as to leave them under dismal apprehensions of something worse to come after. The result was, that they must be parted.

Who can express the torment our lovers felt upon this separation! However, it served only to unite their hearts more firmly; they were but the more eager to see one another. Difficulties increased their desires, and put them upon any attempts without regarding what might be the consequence. *Abelard* finding it impossible to live without his dear *Heloise*, endeavoured to settle a correspondence with her by her maid Agaton, who was a handsome brown girl, well shaped, and likely enough to have pleased a man who was not otherwise engaged. But what a surprise was it to our Doctor, to find this girl refuse his money, and in recompence of the services she was to do him with his mistress, demanded no less a reward than his heart, and making him at once a plain declaration of love! *Abelard* who could love none but *Heloise*, turned from her abruptly, without answering a word. But a rejected woman is a dangerous creature. Agaton knew well how to revenge the affront put upon her, and failed not to acquaint Fulbert with *Abelard's* offers to her, without saying a word how she had been disobliged. Fulbert thought it was time to look about him. He thanked the maid for her care, and entered into measures with her, how to keep *Abelard* from visiting his niece.

The Doctor was now more perplexed than ever: he had no ways left but to apply himself to *Heloise's* singing-master; and the gold which the maid refused prevailed with him. By this means *Abelard* conveyed a letter to *Heloise*, in which he told her, that he intended to come and see her at night, and that the way he had contrived was over the garden-wall by a ladder of cords. This project succeeded, and brought them together. After the first transports of this short interview, *Heloise*, who had found some more than ordinary symptoms within her, acquainted her lover with it. She had informed him of it before by a letter; and now having this opportunity to consult about it; they agreed that she should go to a sister of his in Britany, at whose house she might be privately brought to bed. But before they parted, he endeavored to comfort her, and make her easy in this distress, by giving her assurances of marriage. When *Heloise* heard this proposal she peremptorily rejected it, and gave such reasons [4] for her refusal, as left *Abelard* in the greatest astonishment.

Indeed a refusal of this nature is so extraordinary a thing, that perhaps another instance of it is not to be found in history. I persuade myself, therefore, that I shall not offend my reader, if I make some few remarks upon it. It often happens, that the passion of love stifles or over-rules the rebukes of conscience; but it is unusual for it to extinguish the sensibility of honour. I don't speak of persons of mean birth and no education; but for others, all young women, I suppose, who engage in love-intrigues, flatter themselves with one of these views; either they hope they shall not prove with child, or they shall conceal it from the world, or they shall get themselves married. As for such as resolve to destroy the fruit of their amours, there are but few so void of all natural affections as to be capable of this greatest degree of barbarity. However, this shows plainly, that if Love tyrannizes sometimes, it is such a tyrant as leaves honour in possession of its rights. But *Heloise* had a passion so strong, that she was not at all concerned for her honour or reputation. She was overjoyed to find herself with child, and yet she did her utmost not to be married. Never fore was so odd an example as these two things made when put together. The first was very extraordinary; and how many young women in the world would rather be married to a disagreeable husband than live in a state of reproach? They know the remedy is bad enough, and will cost them dear; but what signifies that, so long as the name of husband hides the flaws made in their honour? But as for *Heloise*, she was not so nice in this point. An excess of passion, never heard of before, made her chuse to be *Abelard's* mistress rather than his wife. We shall see, in the course of this history, how firm she was in this resolution, with what arguments she supported it, and how earnestly she persuaded her gallant to be of the same mind.

Abelard, who was willing to lose no time, least his dear *Heloise* should fall into her uncle's hands, disguised her in the habit of a nun, and sent her away with the greatest dispatch, hoping that after she was brought to bed, he should have more leisure to persuade her to marriage, by which they might screen themselves from the reproach which must otherwise come upon them, as soon as the business should be publickly known.

As soon as *Heloise* was set forward on her journey, *Abelard* resolved to make Fulbert a visit in order to appease him, if possible, and prevent the ill effects of his just indignation.

The news that *Heloise* was privately withdrawn soon made a great noise in the neighbourhood; and reaching Fulbert's ears, filled him with grief and melancholy. Besides, that he had a very tender affection for his niece, and could not live without her, he had the utmost resentment of the affront which *Abelard* had put upon him, by abusing the freedom he had allowed him. This fired him with such implacable fury, as in the end fell heavy upon our poor lovers, and had very dreadful consequences.

When Fulbert saw *Abelard*, and heard from him the reason why *Heloise* was withdrawn, never was man in such a passion. He abandoned himself to the utmost distractions of rage, despair, and thirst of revenge. All the affronts, reproaches, and menaces that could be thought of, were heaped upon *Abelard*; who was, poor man, very passive, and ready to make the Canon all the satisfaction he was able. He gave him leave to say what he pleased; and when he saw that he tired himself with exclaiming, he took up the discourse, and ingenuously confess'd his crime. Then he had recourse to all the prayers, submissions, and promises, he could invent; and begged of him to consider the force of Love, and what foils this tyrant has given to the greatest men: that the occasion of the present misfortunes was the most violent passion that ever was; that this passion continued still; and that he was ready to give both him and his niece all the satisfaction which this sort of injury required. Will you marry her then? said Fulbert, interrupting him. Yes, replied *Abelard*, if you please, and she will consent. If I please! said the Canon, pausing a little; if she will consent! And do you question either? Upon this he was going to offer him his reasons, after his hasty way, why they should be married: But *Abelard* entreated him to suppress his passion a while, and hear what he had to offer: which was, that their marriage might for some time be kept secret. No, says the Canon, the dishonor you have done my niece is public, and the reparation you make her shall be so too, But *Abelard* told him, that since they were to be one family, he hoped he would consider his interest as his own. At last after a great many intreaties, Fulbert seemed content it should be as *Abelard* desired; that he should marry *Heloise* after she was brought to bed, and that in the mean time the business should be kept secret.

Abelard, having given his scholars a vacation, returned into Britany to visit his designed spouse, and to acquaint her with what had passed. She was not at all concerned at her uncle's displeasure; but that which troubled her was, the resolution which she saw her lover had taken to marry her, She endeavoured to dissuade him from it with all the arguments she could think of. She begun with representing to him the wrong he did himself in thinking of marriage: that as she never loved him but for his own sake, she preferred his glory, reputation, and interest, before her own. I know my uncle, said she, will never be pacified with any thing we can do, and what honour shall I get by being your wife, when at the same time I certainly ruin your reputation? What curse may I not justly fear, should I rob the world of so eminent a person as you are? What an injury shall I do the Church? how much shall I disoblige the learned? and what a shame and disparagement will it be to you, whom Nature has fitted for the public good, to devote yourself entirely to a wife? Remember what St. *Paul* says, *Art thou loosed from a wife? seek not a wife.* If neither this great man, not the fathers of the church, can make you change your resolution, consider at least what your philosophers say of it. Socrates has proved, by many arguments, that a wife man ought not to marry. Tully put away his wife Terentia; and when Hircius offered him his sister in marriage he told him, he desired to be excused, because he could never bring himself to divide his thoughts between his books and his wife. In short, said she, how can the study of divinity and philosophy comport with the cries of children, the songs of nurses, and all the hurry of a family? What an odd fight will it be to see maids and scholars, desks and cradles, books and distaffs, pens and spindles, one among another? Those who are rich are never disturbed with the care and charges of housekeeping; but with you scholars it is far otherwise[5].

He that will get an estate must mind the affairs of the world, and consequently is taken off from the study of divinity and philosophy. Observe the conduct of the wife Pagans in this point, who preferred a single life before marriage, and be ashamed that you cannot come up to them. Be more careful to maintain the character and dignity of a philosopher. Don't you know, that there is no action of life which draws after it so sure and long a repentance, and to so little purpose? You fancy to yourself the enjoyments you shall have in being bound to me by a bond which nothing but death can break: but know there is no such thing as sweet chains; and there is a thousand times more glory, honour, and pleasure, in keeping firm to an union which love alone has established, which is supported by mutual esteem and merit, and which owes its continuance to nothing but the satisfaction of seeing each other free. Shall the laws and customs which the gross and carnal world has invented hold us together more surely than the bonds of mutual affection? Take my word for it, you'll see me too often when you see me ev'ry day: you'll have no value for my love nor favours when they are due to you, and cost you no care. Perhaps you don't think of all this at present; but you'll think of nothing else when it will be too late. I don't take notice what the world will say, to see a man in your circumstances get him a wife, and so throw away your reputation, your fortune and your quiet. In short, continued she, the quality of mistress is a hundred times more pleasing to me than that of a wife. Custom indeed, has given a dignity to this latter name, and we are imposed upon by it; but Heaven is my witness, I had rather be *Abelard's* mistress than lawful wife to the Emperor of the whole world. I am very sure I shall always prefer your advantage and satisfaction before my own honour, and all the reputation, wealth, and enjoyments, which the most splendid marriage could bring me. Thus *Heloise* argued, and added a great many more reasons, which I forbear to relate, lest I should tire my reader. It is enough for him to know, that they are chiefly grounded upon her preference of love to marriage, and liberty to necessity.

We might therefore suppose that *Heloise* was afraid lest marriage should prove the tomb of love. The Count de Buffi, who passes for the translator of some of her Letters, makes this to be her meaning, though cloathed in delicate language. But if we examine those which she writ to *Abelard* after their separation, and the expressions she uses to put him in mind, that he was indebted for the passion she had for him to nothing but love itself, we must allow that she had more refined notions, and that never woman was so disinterested. She loved *Abelard* 'tis true; but she declared it was not his sex that she most valued in him.

Some authors [6] are of opinion, that it was not an excess of love which made *Abelard* press *Heloise* to marriage, but only to quiet his conscience: but how can any one tell his reasons for marriage better than he himself? Others say [7] that if *Heloise* did really oppose *Abelard's* design of marrying her so earnestly, it was not because she thought better of concubinage than a married life, but because her affection and respect for her lover leading her to seek his honour and advantage in all things, she was afraid that by marrying him she should stand between him and a bishoprick, which his wit and learning well deserved. But there is no such thing in her Letters, nor in the long account which *Abelard* has left us of the arguments which his mistress used to dissuade him from marriage. These are the faults of many authors, who put such words in the mouths of persons as are most conformable to their own ideas. It is often more advantageous, that a woman should leave her lover free for church dignities, than render him incapable of them by marriage: but is it just therefore to suppose that *Heloise* had any such motives? There is indeed a known story of a man that was possessed of a prebend, and quitted it for a wife. The day after the wedding, he said to his bride, My dear, consider how passionately I loved you, since I lost my preferment to marry you. You have done a very foolish thing, said she; you might have kept that, and have had me notwithstanding.

But to return to our lovers. A modern author, who well understood human nature, has affirmed, "That women by the favours they grant to men, grow she fonder of them; but, on the contrary, the men grow more indifferent[8]." This is not always true, *Abelard* was not the less enamoured with *Heloise* after she had given him the utmost proofs of her love; and their familiarity was so far from having abated his flame, that it seems all the eloquence of *Heloise* could not persuade *Abelard* that he wronged himself in thinking to marry her. He admired the wit, the passion, and the ingenuity of his mistress, but in these things he did not come short of her. He knew so well how to represent to her the necessity of marriage, the discourse which he had about it with Fulbert, his rage if they declined it, and how dangerous it might be to both of them, that at last she consented to do whatever he pleased: but still with an inconceivable reluctance, which showed that she yielded for no other reason but the fear of disobliging him.

Abelard was willing to be near his mistress till she was brought to bed, which in a short time she was of a boy. As soon as *Heloise* was fit to go abroad, *Abelard* carried her to Paris, where they were married in the most private manner that could be, having no other company but Fulbert, and two or three particular friends. However, the wedding quickly came to be known. The news of it was already whispered about; people soon began to talk of it more openly, till at last they mentioned it to the married pair.

Fulbert who was less concerned to keep his word than to cover the reproach of his family, took care to spread it abroad. But *Heloise*, who loved *Abelard* a thousand times better than she did herself, and always valued her dear Doctor's honour above her own, denied it with the most solemn protestations, and did all she could to make the world believe her. She constantly affirmed, that the reports of it were mere slanders; that *Abelard* never proposed any such thing; and if he had, she would never have consented to it. In short, she denied it so constantly, and with such earnestness, that she was generally believed. Many people thought, and boldly affirmed, that the Doctor's enemies had spread this story on purpose to lessen his character. This report came to Fulbert's ears, who, knowing that *Heloise* was the sole author of it, fell into so outrageous a passion at her, that after a thousand reproaches and menaces, he proceeded to use her barbarously. But *Abelard*, who loved her never the worse for being his wife, could not see this many days with patience. He resolved therefore to order matters so as to deliver her from this state of persecution. To this purpose they consulted together what course was to be taken; and agreed, that for setting them both free, her from the power and ill-humour of her uncle, and him from the persecuting reports which went about of him, *Heloise* should retire into a convent, where she should take the habit of a nun, all but the veil, that so she might easily come out again, when they should have a more favourable opportunity. This design was proposed, approved, and executed, almost at the same time. By this means they effectually put a stop to all reports about a marriage. But the Canon was too dangerous a person to be admitted to this consultation; he would never have agreed to their proposal; nor could he hear of it without the utmost rage. 'Twas then that he conceived a new desire of revenge, which he pursued till he had executed it in the most cruel manner imaginable. This retreat of *Heloise* gave him the more sensible affliction, because she was so far from covering her own reputation, that she completed his shame. He considered it as *Abelard's* contrivance, and a fresh instance of his perfidious dealing towards him. And this reflection put him upon studying how to be revenged on them both at one stroke; which, aiming at the root of the mischief, should forever disable them from offending again.

While this plot was in agitation, the lovers, who were not apt to trouble their heads about what might happen, spent their time in the most agreeable manner that could be. *Abelard* could not live long without a sight of his dear wife. He made her frequent visits in the convent of Argenteuil, to which she was retired. The nuns of this abbey enjoyed a very free kind of life: the grates and parlours were open enough. As for *Heloise*, she had such excellent qualifications as made the good sisters very fond of her, and extremely pleased that they had such an amiable companion. And as they were not ignorant what reports there were abroad, that she was married to the famous *Abelard*, (though she denied it to the last,) the most discerning among them, observing the frequent visits of the Doctor, easily imagined that she had reasons for keeping herself private, and so they took her case into consideration, and expressed a wonderful compassion for her misfortunes.

Some of them, whom *Heloise* loved above the rest, and in whom she put great confidence, were not a little aiding and assisting in the private interviews which she had with *Abelard*, and in giving him opportunities to enter the convent. The amorous Doctor made the best use of every thing. The habit which *Heloise* wore the place where he was to see her, the time and seasons proper for his visit, the stratagems which must be used to facilitate his entrance, and carry him undiscovered to *Heloise's* chamber, the difficulties they met with, the reasons they had for not letting it be known who they were, and the fear they were in of being taken together; all this gave their amours an air of novelty, and added to their lawful embraces all the taste of stolen delights.

These excesses had then their charms, but in the end had fatal consequences. The furious Canon persisting in his design of being revenged on *Abelard*, notwithstanding his marriage with his niece, found means to corrupt a domestic of the unfortunate Doctor, who gave admittance into his master's chamber to some assassins hired by Fulbert, who seized him in his sleep, and cruelly deprived him of his manhood, but not his life. The servant and his accomplices fled for it. The wretched *Abelard* raised such terrible outcries, that the people in the house and the neighbours being alarmed, hastened to him, and gave such speedy assistance, that he was soon out of a condition of fearing death.

The news of this accident made great noise, and its singularity raised the curiosity of abundance of persons, who came the next day as in procession, to see, to lament and comfort him. His scholars loudly bewailed his misfortune, and the women distinguished themselves upon this occasion by extraordinary marks of tenderness. And 'tis probable among the great number of ladies who pitied *Abelard*, there were some with whom he had been very intimate: for his philosophy did not make him scrupulous enough to esteem every small infidelity a crime, when it did not lessen his constant love of *Heloise*.

This action of Fulbert was too tragical to pass unpunished: the traiterous servant and one of the assassins were seized and condemned to lose their eyes, and to suffer what they had done to *Abelard*. But Fulbert denying he had any share in the action saved himself from the punishment with the loss only of his benefices. This sentence did not satisfy *Abelard*; he made his complaint to no purpose to the bishop and canons; and if he had made a remonstrance at Rome, where he once had a design of carrying the matter, 'tis probable he would have had no better success. It requires too much money to gain a cause there. One *Foulques*, prior of Deuil, and intimate friend of *Abelard*, wrote thus to him upon the occasion of his misfortune: "If you appeal to the Pope without bringing an immense sum of money, it will be useless: nothing can satisfy the infinite avarice and luxury of the Romans. I question if you have enough for such an undertaking; and if you attempt it, nothing will perhaps remain but the vexation of having flung away so much money. They who go to Rome without large sums to squander away, will return just as they went, the expence of their journey only excepted[9]." But since I am upon Foulques's letters which is too extraordinary to be passed over in silence, I shall give the reader some reflections which may make him amends for the trouble of a new digression.

This friend of *Abelard* lays before him many advantages which might be drawn from his misfortune. He tells him his extraordinary talents, subtilty, eloquence and learning had drawn from all parts an incredible number of auditors, and so filled him with excessive vanity: he hints gently at another thing, which contributed not a little towards making him proud, namely, that the women continually followed him, and gloried in drawing him into their snares. This misfortune, therefore, would cure him of his pride, and free him from those snares of women which had reduced him even to indigence, tho' his profession got him a large revenue; and now he would never impoverish himself by his gallantries.

Heloise herself, in some passages of her *Letters*, says, that there was neither maid nor wife [10], who in *Abelard's* absence did not form designs for him, and in his presence was not inflamed with love: the queens themselves, and ladies of the first quality, envied the pleasures she enjoyed with him. But we are not to take these words of *Heloise* in a strict sense; because as she loved *Abelard* to madness, so she imagined every one else did. Besides, that report, to be sure, hath added to the truth. It is not at all probable that a man of *Abelard's* sense, and who according to all appearance passionately loved his wife, should not be able to contain himself within some bounds, but should squander away all his money upon mistresses, even to his not reserving what was sufficient to provide for his necessities. Foulques owns, that he speaks only upon hearsay, and in that, no doubt, envy, and jealousy had their part.

Foulques tells him besides, that the amputation of a part of his body, of which he made such ill use, would suppress at the same time a great many troublesome passions, and procure him liberty of reflecting on himself, instead of being hurried to and fro by his passions: his meditations would be no more interrupted by the emotions of the flesh, and therefore he would be more successful in discovering the secrets of Nature. He reckons it as a great advantage to him, that he would no more be the terror of husbands, and might now lodge any where without being suspected. And forgets not to acquaint him, that he might converse with the finest women without any fear of those temptations which sometimes overpower even age itself upon the sight of such objects. And, lastly, he would have the happiness of being exempt from the illusions of sleep; which exemption, according to him is a peculiar blessing.

It was with reason that Foulques reckons all these as advantages very extraordinary in the life of an ecclesiastick. It is easy to observe, that, to a person who devotes himself to continence, nothing can be more happy than to be insensible to beauty and love, for they who cannot maintain their chastity but by continual combats are very unhappy. The life of such persons is uneasy, their state always doubtful. They but too much feel the trouble of their warfare; and if they come off victorious in an engagement, it is often with a great many wounds. Even such of them as in a retired life are at the greatest distance from temptations, by continually struggling with their inclinations, setting barriers against the irruptions of the flesh, are in a miserable condition. Their entrenchments are often forced, and their conscience filled with sorrow and anxiety. What progress might one make in the ways of virtue, who is not obliged to fight an enemy for every foot of ground? Had *Abelard's* misfortune made him indeed such as Foulques supposed, we should see him in his *Letters* express his motives of comfort with a better grace. But though he now was in a condition not able to satisfy a passion by which he had suffered so much, yet was he not insensible at the sight of those objects which once gave him so much pleasure. This discourse therefore of Foulques, far from comforting *Abelard* in his affliction, seems capable of producing the contrary effect; and it is astonishing if *Abelard* did not take it so, and think he rather insulted him, and consequently resent it.

As to dreams, St. Austin informs us of the advantage Foulques tells his friend he had gained. St. Austin implores the grace of God to deliver him from this sort of weakness, and says, he gave consent to those things in his sleep which he should abominate awake, and laments exceedingly so great a regaining weakness.

But let us go on with this charitable friend's letter; it hath too near a relation to this to leave any part of it untouched. Matrimonial functions (continues Foulques) and the cares of a family, will not now hinder your application to please God. And what a happiness is it, not to be in a capacity of sinning? And then he brings the examples of Origen, and other martyrs, who rejoice now in heaven for their being upon earth in the condition *Abelard* laments; as if the impossibility of committing a sin could secure any one from desiring to do it. But one of the greatest motives of comfort, and one upon which he insists the most is, because his misfortune is irreparable. This is indeed true in fact, but the consequence of his reasoning is not so certain; *Afflict not yourself* (says he) *because your misfortune is of such a nature as is never to be repaired.*

It must be owned, that the general topics of consolation have two faces, and may therefore be considered very differently, even so as to seem arguments for sorrow. As for instance, one might argue very justly, that a mother should not yield too much to grief upon the loss of a son, because her tears are unavailable; and tho' she should kill herself with sorrow, she can never, by these means, bring her son to life. Yet this very thing, that all she can do is useless, is the main occasion of her grief; she could bear it patiently, could she any ways retrieve her loss. When Solon lamented the death of his son, and some friend, by way of comfort, told him his tears were insignificant. *That*, said he, *is the very reason why I weep.*

But Foulques argues much better afterwards; he says, *Abelard* did not suffer this in the commission of an ill act, but sleeping peaceably in his bed; that is he was not caught in any open fact, such has cost others the like loss. This is indeed a much better topic than the former, though it must be allowed that *Abelard* had drawn this misfortune on himself by a crime as bad as adultery; yet the fault was over, and he had made all the reparation in his power, and when they maimed him he thought no harm to any body.

Abelard's friend makes use likewise of other consolatory reasons in his Letter, and represents to him, after a very moving manner, the part which the Bishop and Canons, and all the Ecclesiasticks of Paris, took in his disgrace, and the mourning there was among the inhabitants and especially the women, upon this occasion. But, in this article of consolation, how comes it to pass that he makes no mention of *Heloise*? This ought not to appear strange: she was the most injured, and therefore questionless, her sorrows were sufficiently known to him; and it would be no news to tell the husband that his wife was in the utmost affliction for him. For as we observed before, though she was in a convent, she had not renounced her husband, and those frequent visits he made her were not spent in reading homilies. But let us make an end of our reflections on Foulques's curious Letter, Foulques, after advising *Abelard* not to think of carrying the matter before the Pope, by assuring him that it required too great expence to obtain any satisfaction at that court, concludes all with this last motive of consolation, that the imagined happiness he had lost was always accompanied with abundance of vexation; but if he persevered in his spirit of resignation, he would, without doubt, at the last day obtain that justice he had now failed of. 'Tis great pity we have not *Abelard's* answer to this delicate Letter, the matter then would look like one of Job's Dialogues with his friends. *Abelard* would generally have enough to reply, and Foulques would often be but a sorry comforter. However, it is certain this Letter was of some weight with *Abelard*; for we find afterwards he never thought of making a voyage to Rome. Resolved to hear his calamity patiently, he left to God the avenging of the cruel and shameful abuse he had suffered.

But let us return to *Heloise*. 'Tis probable her friends of the convent of Argenteuil concealed so heavy a misfortune from her for some time; but at last she heard the fatal news. Though the rage and fury of her uncle threatened her long since with some punishment, yet could she never suspect any thing of this nature. It will be saying too little to tell the reader she felt all the shame and sorrow that is possible. She only can express those violent emotions of her soul upon so severe an occasion.

In all probability this misfortune of *Abelard* would have been a thorough cure of her passion, if we might argue from like cases: but there is no rule so general as not to admit of some exceptions; and *Heloise's* love upon this severe trial proved like Queen Stratonice's, who was not less passionate for her favourite Combabus, when she discovered his impotence, than she had been before.

Shame and sorrow had not less seized *Abelard* than *Heloise*, nor dared he ever appear in the world; so that he resolved, immediately upon his cure, to banish himself from the sight of men, and hide himself in the darkness of a monastick life avoiding all conversation with any kind of persons excepting his dear *Heloise*, by whose company he endeavoured to comfort himself. But she at last resolved to follow his example, and continue forever in the convent of Argenteuil where she was. *Abelard* himself confesses, that shame rather than devotion had made him take the habit of a monk; and that it was jealousy more than love which engaged him to persuade *Heloise* to be professed before he had made his vow. The Letters which follow this history will inform us after what manner and with what resolution they separated. *Heloise* in the twenty-second year of her age generously quitted the world, and renounced all those pleasures she might reasonably have promised herself, to sacrifice herself entirely to the fidelity and obedience she owed her husband, and to procure him that ease of mind which he said he could no otherwise hope for.

Time making *Abelard's* misfortune familiar to him, he now entertained thoughts of ambition, and of supporting the reputation he had gained of the most learned man of the age. He began with explaining the *Acts of the Apostles* to the monks of the monastery of St. *Dennis* to which he had retired; but the disorders of the abbey, and debauchees of the Abbot, which equally with his dignity, were superior to those of the simple monks, quickly drove him hence. He had made himself uneasy to them by censuring their irregularity. They were glad to part with him, and he to leave them.

As soon as he had obtained leave of the Abbot, he retired to Thinbaud in Champaign, where he set up a school, persuading himself that his reputation would bring him a great number of scholars. And indeed they flocked to him, not only from the most distant provinces of Prance, but also from Rome, Spain, England, and Germany, in such number, that the towns could not provide accommodation, nor the country provisions, enough for them[11], But *Abelard* did not foresee, that this success and reputation would at the same time occasion him new troubles. He had made himself two considerable enemies at Laon, Alberic of Rheims, and Lotulf of Lombardy, who, as soon as they perceived how prejudicial his reputation was to their schools, sought all occasions to ruin him; and thought they had a lucky handle to do so from a book of his, intituled, *The Mystery of the Trinity*. This they pretended was heretical, and through the Archbishop's means they procured a council at Soissons in the year 1121; and without suffering *Abelard* to make any defence, ordered his book to be burnt by his own hands, and himself to be confined to the convent of St. Medard. This sentence gave him such grief, that he says himself, the unhappy fate of his writing touched him more sensibly than the misfortune he had suffered through Fulbert's means. Nor was it only his fatherly concern for his own productions, but the indelible mark of heresy which by this means was fixed on him, which so exceedingly troubled him.

That the curious reader may have a complete knowledge of this matter, I shall here give an account of that pretended heresy which was imputed to *Abelard*. The occasion of his writing this book was, that his scholars demanded [12] philosophical arguments on that subject; often urging that it was impossible to believe what was not understood; that it was to abuse the world, to preach a doctrine equally unintelligible to the speaker and auditor; and that it was for the blind to lead the blind. These young men were certainly inclined to Sabellinism. *Abelard's* enemies however did not accuse him of falling into this, but another heresy as bad, Tritheism; though indeed he was equally free from both: he explained the unity of the Godhead by comparisons drawn from human things but according to a passage of St. Bernard[13], one of his greatest enemies, he seemed to hold, that no one ought to believe what he could not give a reason for. However *Abelard's* treatise upon this subject pleased every one except those of his own profession, who, stung with envy that he should find out explanations which they could not have thought of, raised such a cry of heresy upon him, that he and some of his scholars had like to have been stoned by the mob[14]. By their powerful cabals they prevailed with Conan bishop of Preneste, the Pope's legate, who was president of the council, to condemn his book, pretending that he asserted three Gods, which they might easily suggest, when he was suffered to make no defence. 'Tis certain he was very orthodox in the doctrine of the Trinity; and all this process against him was only occasioned by the malice of his enemies. His logical comparison (and logic was his masterpiece) proved rather the three Divine Persons One, than multiplied the Divine Nature into Three. His comparison is, that as the three proportions [15] in a syllogism are but one truth, so the Father, Son, and Holy Ghost, are but one Essence; and it is certain the inconveniences which may be drawn from this parallel are not more than what may be drawn from the comparison of the three dimensions of solids, so much insisted on by the famous orthodox mathematician Dr. Wallis of England. But great numbers of pious and learned divines, who have not been over-subtile in politics, have been persecuted and condemned as well as *Abelard* by the ignorance and malice of their brethren.

A little after his condemnation, *Abelard* was ordered to return to St. Dennis. The liberty he had taken to censure the vicious lives of the monks had raised him a great many enemies. Amongst these was St. Bernard, not upon the same motives as those monks, but because *Abelard's* great wit, joined with so loose and sensual a life, gave him jealousy, who thought it impossible the heart should be defiled without the head being likewise tainted.

Scarce had he returned to St. Dennis, when one day he dropped some words, intimating he did not believe that the St. Dennis their patron was the Areopagite mentioned in the Scripture, there being no probability that he ever was in France. This was immediately carried to the Abbot, who was full of joy, that he had now a handle to heighten the accusations of heresy against him with some crime against the state; a method frequently used by this sort of gentlemen to make sure their revenge. In those times, too, the contradicting the notions of the monks was enough to prove a man an atheist, heretic, rebel, or any thing; learning signified nothing. If any one of a clearer head and larger capacity had the misfortune to be suspected of novelty, there was no way to avoid the general persecution of the monks but voluntarily banishing himself. The Abbot immediately assembled all the house, and declared he would deliver up to the secular power a person who had dared to reflect upon the honour of the kingdom and of the crown. *Abelard* very rightly judging that such threatenings were not to be despised, fled by night to Champaign, to a cloister of the monks of Troies, and there patiently waited till the storm should be over. After the death of this Abbot, which, very luckily for him happened soon after his flight, he obtained leave to live where he pleased, though it was not without using some cunning. He knew the monks of so rich a house had fallen into great excesses, and were very obnoxious to the court, who would not fail to make their profit of it: he therefore procured it should be represented to his council as very disadvantageous to his Majesty's interest, that a person who was continually censuring the lives of his brethren should continue any longer with them. This was immediately understood, and orders given to some great men at court to demand of the Abbot and monks why they kept a person in their house whose conduct was so disagreeable to them; and, far from being an ornament to the society, was a continual vexation, by publishing their faults? This being very opportunely moved to the new Abbot, he gave *Abelard* leave to retire to what cloister he pleased.

Abelard, who indeed had all the qualities which make a great man, could not however bear, without repining, the numerous misfortunes with which he saw himself embarrassed, and had frequent thoughts of publishing a manifesto to justify himself from the scandalous imputations his enemies had laid upon him and to undeceive those whom their malice had prejudiced against him. But upon cooler thought he determined, that it was better to say nothing and to shew them by his silence how unworthy he thought them of his anger. Thus being rather enraged than troubled at the injuries he had suffered, he resolved to found a new society, consisting chiefly of monks. To this purpose he chose a solitude in the diocese of Troies, and upon some ground which was given by permission of the Bishop, he built a little house and a chapel, which he dedicated to the most Holy Trinity.

Men of learning were then scarce, and the desire of science was beginning to spread itself. Our exile was inquired after and found; scholars crowded to him from all parts: they built little huts, and were very liberal to their master for his lectures; content to live on herbs, and roots, and water, that they might have the advantage of learning from so extraordinary a man; and with great zeal they enlarged the chapel building that and their professor's house with wood and stone.

Upon this occasion *Abelard*, to continue the memory of the comfort he had received in this desart, dedicated his new built chapel to the Holy Ghost, by the name of the Paraclete, or Comforter. The envy of Alberic and Lotulf, which had long since persecuted him, was strangely revived, upon seeing so many scholars flock to him from all parts, notwithstanding the inconvenience of the place, and in contempt of the masters who might so commodiously be found in the towns and cities.

They now more than ever sought occasion to trouble him; the name of Paraclete furnished them with one. They gave out that this novelty was a consequence of his former heresy, and that it was no more lawful to dedicate churches to the Holy Ghost than to God the Father: that this title was a subtile art of instilling that poison which he durst not spread openly, and a consequence of his heretical doctrine which had been condemned already by a council. This report raised a great clamour among numbers of people, whom his enemies employed on all sides. But the persecution grew more terrible when St. Bernard and St. Norbet declared against him; two great zealots, fired with the spirit of Reformation, and who declared themselves restorers of the primitive discipline, and had wonderfully gained upon the affections of the populace. They spread such scandal against him that they prejudiced his principal friends, and forced those who still loved him not to shew it any ways; and upon these accounts made his life so bitter to him that he was upon the point of leaving Christendom[16]. But his unhappiness would not let him do a thing which might have procur'd his ease; but made him still continue with Christians, and with monks (as himself expresses it) worse than Heathens[17].

The Duke of Britany, informed of his misfortunes, and of the barbarity of his enemies, named him to the abbey of St. Gildas, in the diocese of Vannes, at the desire of the monks who had already elected him for their superior. Here he thought he had found a refuge from the rage of his enemies, but in reality he had only changed one trouble for another. The profligate lives of the monks, and the arbitrariness of a lord, who had deprived them of the greater part of their revenues, so that they were obliged to maintain their mistresses and children at their own private expence, occasioned him a thousand vexations and dangers. They several times endeavoured to poison him in his ordinary diet, but proving unsuccessful that way, they cried to do it in the holy sacrament. Excommunications, with which he threatened the most mutinous, did not abate the disorder. He now feared the poniard more than poison, and compared his case to his whom the tyrant of Saracuse caused to be seated at his table, with a sword hanging over him, fastened only by a thread.

Whilst *Abelard* thus suffered in his abbey by his monks, the nuns of Argenteuil, of whom *Heloise* was prioress, grew so licentious, that Sugger, abbot of Dennis, taking advantage of their irregularities, got possession of their monastery. He sent the original writings to Rome;

and having obtained the answer he desired, he expelled the nuns, and established in their place monks of his order.

Some censorious people upon reading this passage, will be apt to entertain strong suspicions of *Heloise*, and judge it probable that a governor does not behave well when dissoluteness is known to reign in the society. I have never read that she was included by name in the general scandal of the society, and therefore am cautious not to bring any accusations against her. Our Saviour says, *No one hath condemned thee, neither do I condemn thee*.

Heloise, at her departure from the convent of Argenteuil, applied to her husband; who by permission of the Bishop Troies, gave her the house and chapel of the *Paraclete*, with its appendages; and placing there some nuns, founded a nunnery. Pope Innocent II. confirmed this donation in the year 1131. This is the origin of the abbey of the *Paraclete*, of which *Heloise* was the first abbess. Whatever her conduct was among the licentious nuns of Argenteuil, it is certain she lived so regular in this her new and last retreat, and behaved herself with that prudence, zeal, and piety, that she won the hearts of all the world, and in a small time had abundance of donations. *Abelard* himself says she had more in one year than he could have expected all his life, had he lived there. The bishops loved her as their child, the abbesses as their sister, and the world as their mother. It must be owned some women have had wonderful talents for exciting Christian charity. The abbesses which succeeded *Heloise* have often been of the greatest families in the kingdom. There is a list of them in the *Notes* of *Andrew du Chene* upon *Abelard's* works, from the time of the foundation in 1130, to 1615; but he has not thought fit to take notice of Jane Cabot, who died the 25th of June 1593, and professed the Protestant religion, yet without marrying, or quitting her habit, though she was driven from her abbey.

After *Abelard* had settled *Heloise* here, he made frequent journies from Britany to Champaign, to take care of the interest of this rising house, and to ease himself from the vexations of his own abbey. But slander so perpetually followed this unhappy man, that though his present condition was universally known, he was reproached with a remaining voluptuous passion for his former mistress. He complains of his hard usage in one of his Letters; but comforts himself by the example of St. Jerom, whose friendship with Paula occasioned scandal too; and therefore he entirely confuted this calumny, by remarking that even the most jealous commit their wives to the custody of eunuchs.

The thing which gives the greatest handle to suspect *Heloise's* prudence, and that *Abelard* did not think himself safe with her, is his making a resolution to separate himself forever from her. During his being employed in establishing this new nunnery, and in ordering their affairs, as well temporal as spiritual, he was diligent in persuading her, by frequent and pious admonitions, to such a separation; and insisted, that in order to make their retirement and penitence more profitable, it was absolutely necessary they should seriously endeavour to forget each other, and for the future think on nothing but God. When he had given her directions for her own conduct, and rules for the management of the nuns, he took his last leave of her and returned to his abbey in Britany where he continued a long time without her hearing any mention of him.

By chance, a letter he wrote to one of his friends, to comfort him under some disgrace, wherein he had given him a long account of all the persecutions he himself had suffered, fell into Heloise's hands. She knew by the superscription from whom it came, and her curiosity made her open it. The reading the particulars of a story she was so much concerned in renewed all her passion, and she hence took an occasion to write to him, complaining of his long silence. *Abelard* could not forbear answering her. This occasioned the several Letters between them which follow this History; and in these we may observe how high a woman is capable of railing the sentiments of her heart when possessed of a great deal of wit and learning, at well as a most violent love.

I shall not tire the reader with any farther reflections on the Letters of those two lovers, but leave them entirely to his own judgment; only remarking, that he ought not to be surprised to find *Heloise's* more tender, passionate, and expressive, than those of *Abelard*. She was younger and consequently more ardent than he. The sad condition he was in had not altered her love. Besides, she retired only in complaisance to a man she blindly yielded to; and resolving to preserve her fidelity inviolable, she strove to conquer her desires, and make a virtue of necessity. But the weakness of her sex continually returned, and she felt the force of love in spite of all resistance. It was not the same with *Abelard*; for though it was a mistake to think, that by not being in a condition of satisfying his passion, he was as *Heloise* imagined, wholly delivered from the thorn of sensuality; yet he was truly sorry for the disorders of his past life, he was sincerely penitent, and therefore his Letters are less violent and passionate than those of *Heloise*.

About ten years after *Abelard* had retired to his abbey, where study was his chief business, his enemies, who had resolved to persecute him to the last, were careful not to let him enjoy the ease of retirement. They thought he was not sufficiently plagued with his monks, and therefore brought a new process of heresy against him before the Archbishop of Sens. He desired he might have the liberty of defending his doctrine before a public assembly, and it was granted him. Upon this account the Council of Sens was assembled, in which Louis the VII, assisted in person, in the year 1140. St. Bernard was the accuser, and delivered to the assembly some propositions drawn from *Abelard's* book, which were read in the Council. This accusation gave *Abelard* such fears, and was managed with such inveterate malice by his enemies, and with such great unfairness, in drawing consequences he never thought of, that, imagining he had friends at Rome who would protect his innocence, he made an appeal to the Pope. The Council notwithstanding his appeal, condemned his book, but did not meddle with his person; and gave an account of the whole proceeding to Pope Innocent II. praying him to confirm their sentence. St. Bernard had been so early in prepossessing the Pontiff, that he got the sentence confirmed before *Abelard* heard any thing of it, or had any time to present himself before the tribunal to which he had appealed. His Holiness ordered besides, that *Abelard's* books should be burnt, himself confined, and for ever prohibited from teaching.

This passage of St. Bernard's life is not much for the honour of his memory: and whether he took the trouble himself to extract the condemned propositions from *Abelard's* works, or intrusted it to another hand, it is certain the paper he gave in contained many things which *Abelard* never wrote, and others which he did not mean in the same sense imputed to him.

When a few particular expressions are urged too rigidly, and unthought of consequences drawn from some assertions, and no regard is had to the general intent and scope of an author, it is no difficult matter to find errors in any book. For this reason, Beranger of Poitiers,

Abelard's scholar defended his master against St. Bernard, telling him he ought not to persecute others, whose own writings were not exempt from errors; demonstrating, that he himself had advanced a position which he would not have failed to have inserted in this extract as a monstrous doctrine, if he had found them in the writings of *Abelard.*

Some time after *Abelard's* condemnation, the Pope was appeased at the solicitation of the Abbot of Clugni, who received this unfortunate gentleman into his monastery with great humanity, reconciled him with St. Bernard, and admitted him to be a Religious of his society.

This was *Abelard's* last retirement, in which he found all manner of kindness; he read lectures to the monks, and was equally humble and laborious. At last growing weak, and afflicted with a complication of diseases, he was sent to the priory of St. Marcel upon the Saone, near Chalons, a very agreeable place, where he died the 21st of April 1142, in the 63d year of his age. His corpse was sent to the chapel of *Paraclete*, to *Heloise*, to be interred, according to her former request of him, and to his own desire. The Abbot of Clugni, when he sent the body to *Heloise* according to the custom of those times, sent with it an absolution, to be fixed, together with his epitaph, on his grave-stone, which absolution was at follows:

"I Peter, Abbot of Clugni, having received Father *Abelard* into the number of my Religions, and given leave that his body be privately conveyed to the abbey of the Paraclete, to be disposed of by *Heloise* Abbess of the same abbey; do, by the authority of God and all the saints, absolve the said *Abelard* from all his sins[18]."

Heloise, who survived him twenty years, had all the leisure that could be to effect the cure of her unhappy passion. Alas! she was very long about it! she passed the rest of her days like a religions and devout Abbess, frequent in prayers, and entirely employed in the regulation of her society. She loved study; and being a mistress of the learned languages, the Latin, Greek, and Hebrew, she was esteemed a miracle of learning.

Abelard, in a letter he wrote to the Religious of his new house, says expressly, that *Heloise* understood these three languages. The Abbot of Clugni, likewise, in a letter he wrote to her, tells her, she excelled in learning not only all her sex, but the greatest part of men[19]. And in the calendar of the house of the Paraclete she is recorded in these words: *Heloise, mother and first abbess of this place, famous for her learning and reli-*

gion. I must not here pass by a custom the Religious of the *Paraclete* now have to commemorate how learned their first Abbess was in the Greek, which is, that every year, on the day of Pentecost, they perform divine service in the Greek tongue. What a ridiculous vanity!

Francis d'Amboise tells us how subtilely one day she satisfied St. Bernard, upon asking her, why in her abbey, when they recited the Lord's Prayer, they did not say, *Give us this day our* Daily *bread*, but *Give us this day our* Supersubstantial *bread*, by an argument drawn from the originals, affirming we ought to follow the Greek version of the gospel of St. *Matthew* wrote in *Hebrew*. Without doubt, it was not a little surprising to St. Bernard, to hear a woman oppose him in a controversy, by citing a *Greek* text. 'Tis true, some authors say, *Abelard* made this answer to St. Bernard, after hearing from *Heloise* that objections were made to that form of prayer. However the case was, a woman with a small competency of learning might in those time pass for a miracle; and though she might not equal those descriptions which have been given of her, yet she may deservedly be placed in the rank of women of the greatest learning. Nor was she less remarkable for her piety, patience, and resignation, during her sicknesses in the latter part of her life. She died the 17th of May 1163. 'Tis said she desired to be buried in the same tomb with her *Abelard*, though that probably was not executed. Francis d'Amboise says, he saw at the convent the tombs of the founder and foundress near together. However a manuscript of Tours gives us an account of an extraordinary miracle which happened when *Abelard*'s grave was opened for *Heloise*'s body, namely that *Abelard* stretched out his arms to receive her, and embraced her closely, though there were twenty good years passed since he died. But that is a small matter to a writer of miracles.

I shall conclude this history with an epitaph on *Abelard*, which the Abbot of Clugni sent *Heloise*, and which is now to be read on his tomb; it hath nothing in it delicate either for thought or language, and will scarcely bear a translation. It is only added here for the sake of the curious, and as an instance of the respect paid to the memory of so great a man, and one whom envy had loaded with the greatest defamations.

> *"Petrus in hac petra latitat, quem mundus Homerum*
> *Clamabat, fed jam sidera sidus habent.*

Sol erat hic Gallis, sed eum jam fata tulerunt:
Ergo caret Regio Gallica sole suo.
Ille sciens quid quid fuit ulli scibile, vicit
Artifices, artes absque docente docens.
Undecimae Maij petrum rapuere Calendae,
Privantes Logices atria Rege fuo.
Est fatis, in tumulo Petrus hic jacit Abaelardus,
Cui soli patuit scibile quid quid erat.

Gallorum Socrates, Plato maximus Hesperianum
Noster Aristoteles, Logicis (quicumque fuerunt)
Aut par aut melior; studioium cognitus orbi
Princeps, ingeuio varius, subtilius & acer,
Omnia vi superans rationis & arte loquendi,
Abaelardus erat. Sed nunc magis omnia vincit.
Cum Cluniacensem monacum, moremque professus,
Ad Christi veram transivit philosophiam,
In qua longaevae bene complens ultima vitae,
Philosophis quandoque bonis se connumerandum
Spem dedit, undenas Maio renovante Calendas."

---

1. Papyr. Maffo. Annal. 1. 3. *Joannes Canonicus Pariflus, Heloysiam naturalem filiam habehat prastanti ingenio formaque.*

2. *Tanti quippe tune nominis eram & juventutis & forma gratia praeminebam, ut quamcunque foeminartn nostre dignarer amore nullam verer repulsam.* 1 Epist. Abel. p. 10. Abel.

3.

4. See *Abelard's* letter to *Philintus,* and *Heloise's* first *Letter to Abelard.*

5. *Heloissa dehortabat me nuptiis. Nuptia non conveniunt cum philosophia,* &c. Oper. Abel. p 14.

6. *D'ctionnaire de Moreri*

7. *Fran. d'Amboise.*

8. *M. de la Bruyere.*

9. *This Letter is extant in* Latin *in Abelard's Works.*

10. *Qua conjugata, que virgo non concupiscebat absentem, & non exardescebat in presentem? Qua regina, vel prapotens foemina gaudiis meis non invidebat, vel thalamis?*

11. *Ad quas scholas tanta scholarium multitudo confluxit ut nec locus hospitiis, nec terra sufficeret alimentis.* Abel. Oper. p. 19

12. *Humanas & philosophicas rationes requirebant. & plus quae inteligi, quam quae dici poffenter, efflagitabant.* Abel Op.

13. *Benardi Epist.* 190.

14. *Ita me in clero & populo diffamaverunt, ut pene me populos paucosque qui advenerant ex discipulis nostris prima die nostri anventus lapidarent; dicentes me tres Deos praedicare & scripsisse, sicut ipsis persuasum fuerat.* Abel Oper. p. 20.

15. *Sicut eadem oratio est, propositio, assumptio & conuclusio, ita eadem Essentia est Pater, Filius, and Spiritus Sanctis.* Ibid.

16. *Saepe autem (Deus scit) in tantam lapsus sum desperationem ut Christianorum finibus excessis, ad Gentes transire disponerem, atque ibi quiete sub quacunque tributi pactione inter inimicos Christi christiane vivere.* Abel Op. p. 32.

17. *Incedi in Christianos atque monachos Gentibus longe saeviores atque pejores.* Abel Op. p. 20.

18. *Ego Petrus Cluniacensis Abbas, qui Pet. Abselardum in monacum Cluniacensem recepi, & corpus ejus surtim delatum Heloissa abbatissae & monialibus Paracleti concessi, authoritate omnipotentis Dei & omnium sanctorum, absolvo eum pro officio ab omnibus peccatis suis.*

19. *Studio tuo & mulieres omnes eviciti, & pene viros universos suparasti.* Abel Op.

LETTER I.

ABELARD TO PHILINTUS.

It may be proper to acquaint the reader, that the following Letter was written by *Abelard* to a friend, to comfort him under some afflictions which had befallen him, by a recital of his own sufferings, which had been much heavier. It contains a particular account of his amour with *Heloise*, and the unhappy consequences of it. This Letter was written several years after *Abelard's* separation from *Heloise*.

The last time we were together, *Philintus*, you gave me a melancholy account of your misfortunes. I was sensibly touched with the relation, and, like a true friend, bore a share in your griefs. What did I not say to stop your tears? I laid before you all the reasons Philosophy could furnish, which I thought might any ways soften the strokes of Fortune: but all endeavours have proved useless: grief I perceive, has wholly seized your spirits: and your prudence, far from assisting, seems quite to have forsaken you. But my skilful friendship has found out an expedient to relieve you. Attend to me a moment; hear but the story of my misfortunes, and yours, *Philintus*, will be nothing, if you compare them with those of the loving and unhappy *Abelard*. Observe, I beseech you, at what expence I endeavour to serve you: and think this no small mark of my affection;

for I am going to present you with the relation of such particulars, as it is impossible for me to recollect without piercing my heart with the most sensible affliction.

You know the place where I was born; but not perhaps that I was born with those complexional faults which strangers charge upon our nation, an extreme lightness of temper, and great inconstancy. I frankly own it, and shall be as free to acquaint you with those good qualities which were observed in me. I had a natural vivacity and aptness for all the polite arts. My father was a gentleman, and a man of good parts; he loved the wars, but differed in his sentiments from many who followed that profession. He thought it no praise to be illiterate, but in the camp he knew how to converse at the same time with the Muses and Bellona. He was the same in the management of his family, and took equal care to form his children to the study of polite learning as to their military exercises. As I was his eldest, and consequently his favourite son, he took more than ordinary care of my education. I had a natural genius to study, and made an extraordinary progress in it. Smitten with the love of books, and the praises which on all sides were bestowed upon me, I aspired to no reputation but what proceeded from learning. To my brothers I left the glory of battles, and the pomp of triumphs; nay more, I yielded them up my birthright and patrimony. I knew necessity was the great spur to study, and was afraid I should not merit the title of Learned, if I distinguished myself from others by nothing but a more plentiful fortune. Of all the sciences, Logic was the most to my taste. Such were the arms I chose to profess. Furnished with the weapons of reasoning, I took pleasure in going to public disputations to win trophies; and wherever I heard that this art flourished, I ranged like another Alexander, from province to province, to seek new adversaries, with whom I might try my strength.

The ambition I had to become formidable in logic led me at last to Paris, the centre of politeness, and where the science I was so smitten with had usually been in the greatest perfection. I put myself under the direction of one *Champeaux* a professor, who had acquired the character of the most skilful philosopher of his age, by negative excellencies only, by being the least ignorant. He received me with great demonstrations of kindness, but I was not so happy as to please him long: I was too knowing in the subjects he discoursed upon. I often confuted his notions: often in our disputations I pushed a good argument so home, that all his subtilty was not able to elude its force. It was impossible he should see himself surpassed by his scholar without resentment. It is sometimes dangerous to have too much merit.

Envy increased against me proportionably to my reputation. My enemies endeavoured to interrupt my progress, but their malice only provoked my courage; and measuring my abilities by the jealousy I had raised, I thought I had no farther occasion for Champeaux's lectures, but rather that I was sufficiently qualified to read to others. I stood for a place which was vacant at Melun. My master used all his artifice to defeat my hopes, but in vain; and on this occasion I triumphed over his cunning, as before I had done over his learning. My lectures were always crouded, and beginnings so fortunate, that I entirely obscured the renown of my famous master. Flushed with these happy conquests, I removed to Corbeil to attack the masters there, and so establish my character of the ablest Logician, the violence of travelling threw me into a dangerous distemper, and not being able to recover my strength, my physician, who perhaps were in a league with Champeaux, advised me to retire to my native air. Thus I voluntarily banished myself for some years. I leave you to imagine whether my absence was not regretted by the better sort. At length I recovered my health, when I received news that my greatest adversary had taken the habit of a monk. You may think was an act of penitence for having persecuted me; quite contrary, it was ambition; he resolved to raise himself to some church-dignity therefore he fell into the beaten track, and took on him the garb of feigned austerity; for this is the easiest and and shortest way to the highest ecclesiastical dignities. His wishes were successful, and he obtained a bishoprick: yet did he not quit Paris, and the care of the schools. He went to his diocese to gather in his revenues, but returned and passed the rest of his time in reading lectures to those few pupils which followed him. After this I often-engaged with him, and may reply to you as Ajax did to the Greeks;

> *"If you demand the fortune of that day,*
> *When stak'd on this right hand your honours lay*
> *If I did not oblige the foe to yield,*
> *Yet did I never basely quit the field."*

About this time my father Beranger, who to the age of sixty had lived very agreeably, retired from the world and shut himself up in a cloister, where he offered up to Heaven the languid remains of a life he could make no farther use of. My mother, who was yet young, took the same resolution. She turned a Religious, but did not entirely abandon the satisfactions of life. Her friends were continually at the grate; and the monastery, when one has an inclination to make it so, is exceeding charming and pleasant. I was present when my mother was professed. At my return I resolved to study divinity, and inquired for a director in that study. I was recommended to one *Anselm*, the very oracle of his time; but to give you my own opinion, one more venerable for his age and wrinkles than for his genius or learning. If you consulted him upon any difficulty, the sure consequence was to be much more uncertain in the point. Those who only saw him admired him, but those who reasoned with him were extremely dissatisfied. He was a great master of words, and talked much, but meant nothing. His discourse was a fire, which, instead of enlightening, obscured every thing with its smoke; a tree beautified with variety of leaves and branches, but barren. I came to him with a desire to learn, but found him like the fig-tree in the Gospel, or the old oak to which Lucan compares Pompey. I continued not long underneath his shadow. I took for my guides the primitive Fathers, and boldly launched into the ocean of the Holy Scriptures. In a short time I made such a progress, that others chose me for their director. The number of my scholars were incredible, and the gratuities I received from them were answerable to the great reputation I had acquired. Now I found myself safe in the harbour; the storms were passed, and the rage of my enemies had spent itself without effect. Happy, had I known to make a right use of this calm! But when the mind is most easy, it is most exposed to love, and even security here is the most dangerous state.

And now, my friend, I am going to expose to you all my weaknesses. All men, I believe, are under a necessity of paying tribute, at some time or other, to Love, and it is vain to strive to avoid it. I was a philosopher, yet this tyrant of the mind triumphed over all my wisdom; his darts were of greater force than all my reasoning, and with a sweet constraint he led me whither he pleased. Heaven, amidst an abundance of blessings with which I was intoxicated, threw in a heavy affliction. I became a most signal example of its vengeance; and the more unhappy, because having deprived me of the means of accomplishing my satis-

faction, it left me to the fury of my criminal desires. I will tell you, my
dear friend, the particulars of my story, and leave you to judge whether
I deserved so severe a correction. I had always an aversion for those
light women whom it is a reproach to pursue; I was ambitious in my
choice, and wished to find some obstacles, that I might surmount
them with the greater glory and pleasure.

There was in Paris a young creature, (ah! *Philintus*!) formed in a
prodigality of Nature, to show mankind a finished composition; dear
Heloise! the reputed niece of one *Fulbert* a canon. Her wit and her
beauty would have fired the dullest and most insensible heart; and her
education was equally admirable. *Heloise* was a mistress of the most
polite arts. You may easily imagine that this did not a little help to
captivate me. I saw her; I loved her; I resolved to endeavour to gain
her affections. The thirst of glory cooled immediately in my heart, and
all my passions were lost in this new one. I thought of nothing but
Heloise; every thing brought her image to my mind. I was pensive, restless; and my passion was so violent as to admit of no restraint. I was
always vain and presumptive; I flattered myself already with the most
bewitching hopes. My reputation had spread itself every where; and
could a virtuous lady resist a man that had confounded all the learned
of the age? I was young;—could she show an infallibility to those vows
which my heart never formed for any but herself? My person was
advantageous enough and by my dress no one would have suspected
me for a Doctor; and dress you know, is not a little engaging with
women. Besides, I had wit enough to write a *billet doux*, and hoped, if
ever she permitted my absent self to entertain her, she would read with
pleasure those breathings of my heart.

Filled with these notions, I thought of nothing but the means to
speak to her. Lovers either find or make all things easy. By the offices
of common friends I gained the acquaintance of Fulbert. And, can you
believe it, *Philintus?* he allowed me the privilege of his table, and an
apartment in his house. I paid him, indeed, a considerable sum; for
persons of his character do nothing without money. But what would I
not have given! You my dear friend, know what love is; imagine then
what a pleasure it must have been to a heart so inflamed as mine to be
always so near the dear object of desire! I would not have exchanged
my happy condition for that of the greatest monarch upon earth. I saw
Heloise, I spoke to her: each action, each confused look, told her the

trouble of my soul. And she, on the other side, gave me ground to hope for every thing from her generosity. Fulbert desired me to instruct her in philosophy; by this means I found opportunities of being in private with her and yet I was sure of all men the most timorous in declaring my passion.

As I was with her one day, alone, Charming *Heloise*, said I, blushing, if you know yourself, you will not be surprised with what passion you have inspired me with. Uncommon as it is, I can express it but with the common terms;—I love you, adorable *Heloise*! Till now I thought philosophy made us masters, of all our passions, and that it was a refuge from the storms in which weak mortals are tossed and ship-wrecked; but you have destroyed my security, and broken this philosophic courage. I have despised riches; honour and its pageantries could never raise a weak thought in me; beauty alone hath fired my soul. Happy, if she who raised this passion kindly receives the declaration; but if it is an offence—No, replied *Heloise*; she must be very ignorant of your merit who can be offended at your passion. But, for my own repose, I wish either that you had not made this declaration, or that I were at liberty not to suspect your sincerity. Ah, divine *Heloise*, said I, flinging myself at her feet, I swear by yourself—I was going on to convince her of the truth of my passion, but heard a noise, and it was Fulbert. There was no avoiding it, but I must do a violence to my desire, and change the discourse to some other subject. After this I found frequent opportunities to free *Heloise* from those suspicions which the general insincerity of men had raised in her; and she too much desired what I said were truth, not to believe it. Thus there was a most happy understanding between us. The same house, the same love, united our persons and our desires. How many soft moments did we pass together! We took all opportunities to express to each other our mutual affections, and were ingenious in contriving incidents which might give us a plausible occasion for meeting. Pyramus and Thisbe's discovery of the crack in the wall was but a slight representation of our love and its sagacity. In the dead of night, when Fulbert and his domestics were in a sound sleep, we improved the time proper to the sweets of love. Not contenting ourselves, like those unfortunate loves, with giving insipid kisses to a wall, we made use of all the moments of our charming interviews. In the place where we met we had no lions to fear, and the study of philosophy served us for a blind.

But I was so far from making any advances in the sciences that I lost all my taste of them; and when I was obliged to go from the sight of my dear mistress to my philosophical exercises, it was with the utmost regret and melancholy. Love is incapable of being concealed; a word, a look, nay silence, speaks it. My scholars discovered it first: they saw I had no longer that vivacity thought to which all things were easy: I could now do nothing but write verses to sooth my passion. I quitted Aristotle and his dry maxims, to practise the precepts of the more ingenious Ovid. No day passed in which I did not compose amorous verses. Love was my inspiring Apollo. My songs were spread abroad, and gained me frequent applauses. Those whom were in love as I was took a pride in learning them; and, by luckily applying my thoughts and verses, have obtained favours which, perhaps, they could not otherwise have gained. This gave our amours such an *eclat*, that the loves of *Heloise* and *Abelard* were the subject of all conversations.

The town-talk at last reached Fulbert's ears. It was with great difficulty he gave credit to what he heard, for he loved his niece, and was prejudiced in my favour; but, upon closer examination, he began to be less incredulous. He surprised us in one of our more soft conversations. How fatal, sometimes, are the consequences of curiosity! The anger of Fulbert seemed to moderate on this occasion, and I feared in the end some more heavy revenge. It is impossible to express the grief and regret which filled my soul when I was obliged to leave the canon's house and my dear *Heloise*. But this separation of our persons the more firmly united our minds; and the desperate condition we were reduced to, made us capable of attempting any thing.

My intrigues gave me but little shame, so lovingly did I esteem the occasion. Think what the gay young divinities said, when Vulcan caught Mars and the goddess of Beauty in his net, and impute it all to me. Fulbert surprised me with *Heloise*, and what man that had a soul in him would not have borne any ignominy on the same conditions? The next day I provided myself of a private lodging near the loved house, being resolved not to abandon my prey. I continued some time without appearing publickly. Ah, how long did those few moments seem to me! When we fall from a state of happiness, with what impatience do we bear our misfortunes!

It being impossible that I could live without seeing *Heloise*, I endeavoured to engage her servant, whose name was *Agaton*, in my interest. She was brown, well shaped, a person superior to the ordinary rank; her features regular, and her eyes sparkling; fit to raise love in any man whose heart was not prepossessed by another passion. I met her alone, and intreated her to have pity on a distressed lover. She answered, she would undertake any thing to serve me, but there was a reward.—At these words I opened my purse and showed the shining metal, which lays asleep guards, forces away through rocks, and softens the hearts of the most obdurate fair. You are mistaken, said she, smiling, and shaking her head—you do not know me. Could gold tempt me, a rich abbot takes his nightly station, and sings under my window: he offers to send me to his abbey, which, he says, is situate in the most pleasant country in the world. A courtier offers me a considerable sum of money, and assures me I need have no apprehensions; for if our amours have consequences, he will marry me to his gentleman, and give him a handsome employment. To say nothing of a young officer, who patroles about here every night, and makes his attacks after all imaginable forms. It must be Love only which could oblige him to follow me; for I have not like your great ladies, any rings or jewels to tempt him: yet, during all his siege of love, his feather and his embroidered coat have not made any breach in my heart. I shall not quickly be brought to capitulate, I am too faithful to my first conqueror—and then she looked earnestly on me. I answered, I did not understand her discourse. She replied, For a man of sense and gallantry you have a very slow apprehension; I am in love with you *Abelard*. I know you adore *Heloise*, I do not blame you; I desire only to enjoy the second place in your affections. I have a tender heart as well as my mistress; you may without difficulty make returns to my passion. Do not perplex yourself with unfashionable scruples; a prudent man ought to love several at the same time; if one should fail, he is not then left unprovided.

You cannot imagine, *Philintus*, how much I was surprised at these words. So entirely did I love *Heloise* that without reflecting whether Agaton spoke any thing reasonable or not, I immediately left her. When I had gone a little way from her I looked back, and saw her biting her nails in the rage of disappointment, which made me fear some fatal consequences. She hastened to Fulbert, and told him the offer I had made her, but I suppose concealed the other part of the story. The Canon never forgave this affront. I afterwards perceived he was more deeply concerned for his niece than I at first imagined. Let

no lover hereafter follow my example, A woman rejected is an outrageous creature. Agaton was day and night at her window on purpose to
keep me at a distance from her mistress, and so gave her own gallants
opportunity enough to display their several abilities.

I was infinitely perplexed what course to take; at last I applied to
Heloise singing-master. The shining metal, which had no effect on
Agaton, charmed him; he was excellently qualified for conveying a
billet with the greatest dexterity and secrecy. He delivered one of mine
to *Heloise*, who, according to my appointment was ready at the end of a
garden, the wall of which I scaled by a ladder of ropes. I confess to you
all my failings, *Philintus*. How would my enemies, Champeaux and
Anselm, have triumphed, had they seen the redoubted philosopher in
such a wretched condition? Well—I met my soul's joy, my *Heloise*. I
shall not describe our transports, they were not long; for the first news
Heloise acquainted me with plunged me in a thousand distractions. A
floating *delos* was to be sought for, where she might be safely delivered
of a burthen she began already to feel. Without losing much time in
debating, I made her presently quit the Canon's house, and at break of
day depart for Britany; where, she like another goddess, gave the world
another Apollo, which my sister took care of.

This carrying off *Heloise* was sufficient revenge upon Fulbert. It
filled him with the deepest concern, and had like to have deprived him
of all the little share of wit which Heaven had allowed him. His sorrow
and lamentation gave the censorious an occasion of suspecting him for
something more than the uncle of *Heloise*.

In short, I began to pity his misfortune, and think this robbery
which love had made me commit was a sort of treason. I endeavoured
to appease his anger by a sincere confession of all that was past, and by
hearty engagements to marry *Heloise* secretly. He gave me his consent
and with many protestations and embraces confirmed our reconcilia-
tion. But what dependence can be made on the word of an ignorant
devotee. He was only plotting a cruel revenge, as you will see by what
follows.

I took a journey into Britany, in order to bring back my dear
Heloise, whom I now considered as my wife. When I had acquainted
her with what had passed between the Canon and me, I found she was
of a contrary opinion to me. She urged all that was possible to divert
me from marriage: that it was a bond always fatal to a philosopher;

that the cries of children, and cares of a family, were utterly inconsistent with the tranquility and application which the study of philosophy required. She quoted to me all that was written on the subject by Theophrastus, Cicero, and, above all, insisted on the unfortunate Socrates, who quitted life with joy, because by that means he left Xantippe. Will it not be more agreeable to me, said she, to see myself your mistress than your wife? and will not love have more power than marriage to keep our hearts firmly united? Pleasures tasted sparingly, and with difficulty, have always a higher relish, while every thing, by being easy and common, grows flat and insipid.

I was unmoved by all this reasoning. *Heloise* prevailed upon my sister to engage me. Lucille (for that was her name) taking me aside one day, said, What do you intend, brother? Is it possible that *Abelard* should in earnest think of marrying *Heloise?* She seems indeed to deserve a perpetual affection; beauty, youth, and learning, all that can make a person valuble, meet in her. You may adore all this if you please; but not to flatter you, what is beauty but a flower, which may be blasted by the least fit of sickness? When those features, with which you have been so captivated, shall be sunk, and those graces lost, you will too late repent that you have entangled yourself in a chain, from which death only can free you. I shall see you reduced to the married man's only hope of survivorship. Do you think learning ought to make *Heloise* more amiable? I know she is not one of those affected females who are continually oppressing you with fine speeches, criticising books, and deciding upon the merit of authors, When such a one is in the fury of her discourse, husbands, friends, servants, all fly before her. *Heloise* has not this fault; yet it is troublesome not to be at liberty to use the least improper expression before a wife, that you bear with pleasure from a mistress.

But you say, you are sure of the affections of *Heloise* I believe it; she has given you no ordinary proofs. But can you be sure marriage will not be the tomb of her love? The name of Husband and Master are always harsh, and *Heloise* will not be the phenix you now think her. Will she not be a woman? Come, come, the head of a philosopher is less secure than those of other men. My sister grew warm in the argument, and was going to give me a hundred more reasons of this kind; but I angrily interrupted her, telling her only, that she did not know *Heloise.*

A few days after, we departed together from Britany, and came to

Paris, where I completed my project. It was my intent my marriage should be kept secret, and therefore *Heloise* retired among the nuns of Argenteuil.

I now thought Fulbert's anger disarmed; I lived in peace: but, alas! our marriage proved but a weak defence against his revenge. Observe, *Philintus*, to what a barbarity he pursued it! He bribed my servants; an assassin came into my bed chamber by night with a razor in his hand, and found me in a deep sleep. I suffered the most shameful punishment that the revenge of an enemy could invent; in short without losing my life, I lost my manhood. I was punished indeed in the offending part; the desire was left me, but not the possibility of satisfying the passion. So cruel an action escaped not unpunished; the villain suffered the same infliction; poor comfort for so irretrievable an evil; I confess to you, shame, more than any sincere penitence; made me resolve to hide myself from my *Heloise*. Jealousy took possession of my mind; at the very expence of her happiness I decreed to disappoint all rivals. Before I put myself in a cloister, I obliged her to take the habit, and retire into the nunnery of Argenteuil. I remember somebody would have opposed her making such a cruel sacrifice of herself, but she answered in the words of Cornelia, after the death of Pompey the Great;

> *"—O conjux, ego te scelereta peremi,*
> *—Te fata extrema petente*
> *Vita digna fui? Moriar——&c.*

> *O my lov'd lord! our fatal marriage draws*
> *On thee this doom, and I the guilty cause!*
> *Then whilst thou go'st th' extremes of Fate to prove,*
> *I'll share that fate, and expiate thus my love."*

Speaking these verses, she marched up to the altar, and took the veil with a constancy which I could not have expected in a woman who had so high a taste of pleasure which she might still enjoy. I blushed at my own weakness; and without deliberating a moment longer, I buried myself in a cloister, resolving to vanquish a fruitless passion. I now reflected that God had chastised me thus grievously, that he might save me from that destruction in which I had like to have been swallowed up. In order to avoid idleness, the unhappy incendiary of those criminal flames which had ruined me in the world, I endeavoured in my retirement to put those talents to a good use which I had before so much abused. I gave the novices rules of divinity agreeable to the holy fathers and councils. In the mean while, the enemies which my fame had raised up, and especially Alberic and Lotulf, who after the death of their masters Champeaux and Anselm affirmed the sovereignty of learning, began to attack me. They loaded me with the falsest imputations, and, notwithstanding all my defence, I had the mortification to see my books condemned by a council and burnt. This was a cutting sorrow, and, believe me, *Philintus*, the former calamity suffered by the cruelty of Fulbert was nothing in comparison to this.

The affront I had newly received, and the scandalous debaucheries of the monks, obliged me to banish myself, and retire near Nogent. I lived in a desart, where I flattered myself I should avoid fame, and be secure from the malice of my enemies. I was again deceived. The desire of being taught by me, drew crowds of auditors even thither. Many left the towns and their houses, and came and lived in tents; for herbs, coarse fare, and hard lodging, they abandoned the delicacies of a plentiful table and easy life. I looked like a prophet in the wilderness attended by his disciples. My lectures were perfectly clear from all that had been condemned. And happy had it been if our solitude had been inaccessible to Envy! With the considerable gratuities I received I built a chapel, and dedicated it to the Holy Ghost, by the name of the Paraclete. The rage of my enemies now awakened again, and forced me to quit this retreat. This I did without much difficulty. But first the Bishop of Troies gave me leave to establish there a nunnery, which I did, and committed the care of it to my dear *Heloise*. When I had settled her here, can you believe it, *Philintus*? I left her without taking any leave. I did not wander long without settled habitation; for the Duke of Britany, informed of my misfortunes, named me to the Abbey of *Guildas*, where I now am, and where I now suffer every day fresh persecutions.

I live in a barbarous country, the language of which I do not understand. I have no conversation with the rudest people. My walks are on the inaccessible shore of a sea which is perpetually stormy. My monks are known by their dissoluteness, and living without rule or order. Could you see the abbey *Philintus*, you would not call it one. The doors and walls are without any ornament except the heads of wild boars and hinds' feet, which are nailed up against them, and the heads of frightful animals. The cells are hung with the skins of deer. The monks have not so much as a bell to wake them; the cocks and dogs supply that defect. In short, they pass their whole days in hunting; would to Heaven that were their greatest fault, or that their pleasures terminated there! I endeavour in vain to recall them to their duty; they all combine against me, and I only expose myself to continual vexations and dangers. I imagine that every moment a naked sword hang over my head. Sometimes they surround me and load me with infinite abuses; sometimes they abandon me, and I am left alone to my own tormenting thoughts. I make it my endeavour to merit by my sufferings, and to appease an angry God. Sometimes I grieve for the house of the *Paraclete*, and wish to see it again. Ah, *Philintus*! does not the love of *Heloise* still burn in my heart? I have not yet triumphed over that happy passion. In the midst of my retirement I sigh, I weep, I pine, I speak the dear name of *Heloise*, pleased to hear the sound, I complain of the severity of Heaven. But, oh! let us not deceive ourselves: I have not made a right use of grace. I am thoroughly wretched. I have not yet torn from my heart deep roots which vice has planted in it. For if my conversion was sincere, how could I take a pleasure to relate my past follies? Could I not more easily comfort myself in my afflictions? Could I not turn to my advantage those words of God himself, *If they have persecuted me, they will also persecute you; if the world hate you, ye know that it hated me also?* Come *Philintus*, let us make a strong effort, turn our misfortunes to our advantage, make them meritorious, or at least wipe out our offences; let us receive, without murmuring, what comes from the hand of God, and let us not oppose our will to his. Adieu. I give you advice, which could I myself follow, I should be happy.

LETTER II.

HELOISE TO ABELARD.

The foregoing Letter would probably not have produced any others, if it had been delivered to the person to whom it was directed; but falling by accident into *Heloise's* hands, who knew the character she opened it and read it; and by that means her former passion being awakened, she immediately set herself to write to her husband as follows.

To her Lord, her Father; her Husband, her Brother; his Servant his Child; his Wife, his Sister; and to express all that is humble, respectful and loving to her *Abelard*, *Heloise* writes this.[1]

A consolatory letter of yours to a friend happened some days since to fall into my hands. My knowledge of the character, and my love of the hand, soon gave me the curiosity to open it. In justification of the liberty I took, I flattered myself I might claim a sovereign privilege over every thing which came from you nor was I scrupulous to break thro' the rules of good breeding, when it was to hear news of *Abelard*. But how much did my curiosity cost me? what disturbance did it occasion? and how was I surprised to find the whole letter filled with a particular and melancholy account of our misfortunes? I met with my name a hundred times; I never saw it without fear: some heavy calamity always, followed it, I saw yours too, equally unhappy. These mournful but dear remembrances, puts my spirits into such a violent motion, that I thought it was too much to offer comfort to a friend for a few slight disgraces by such extraordinary means, as the representation of our sufferings and revolutions. What reflections did I not make, I began to consider the whole afresh, and perceived myself pressed with the same weight of grief as when we first began to be miserable. Tho' length of time ought to have closed up my wounds, yet the seeing them described by your hand was sufficient to make them all open and bleed afresh. Nothing can ever blot from my memory what you have suffered in defence of your writings. I cannot help thinking of the rancorous malice of Alberic and Lotulf. A cruel uncle and an injured lover, will be always present to my aking sight. I shall never forget what enemies your learning, and what envy your glory, raised against you. I shall never forget your reputation, so justly acquired, torn to pieces, and blasted by the inexorable cruelty of half-learned pretenders to science. Was not your Treatise of Divinity condemned to be burnt? Were you not threatened with perpetual imprisonment? In vain you urged in your defence, that your enemies imposed on you opinions quite different from your meaning; in vain you condemned those opinions; all was of no effect towards your justification; it was resolved you should be a heretic. What did not those two false prophets[2] accuse you of, who declaimed so severely against you before the Council of Sens? What scandals were vented on occasion of the name Paraclete given to your chapel? What a storm was raised against you by the treacherous monks, when you did them the honour to be called their Brother? This history of our numerous misfortunes, related in so true and moving a manner, made my heart bleed within me. My tears, which I could not restrain, have blotted half your letter: I wish they had effaced the whole and that I had returned it to you in that condition. I should then have been satisfied with the little time; kept it, but it was demanded of me too soon.

I must confess I was much easier in my mind before I read your letter. Sure all the misfortunes of lovers are conveyed to them thro' their eyes. Upon reading your letter I felt all mine renewed, I reproached myself for having been so long without venting my sorrows, when the rage of our unrelenting enemies still burns with the same fury. Since length of time, which disarms the strongest hatred, seems but to aggravate theirs; since it is decreed that your virtue shall be persecuted till it takes refuge in the grave, and even beyond that, your ashes perhaps, will not be suffered to rest in peace,—let me always meditate on your calamities, let me publish them thro' all the world, if possible, to shame an age that has not known how to value you. I will spare no one, since no one would interest himself to protect you, and your enemies are never weary of oppressing your innocence, Alas! my memory is perpetually filled with bitter remembrances of past evils, and are there more to be feared still? shall my *Abelard* be never mentioned without tears? shall thy dear name be never spoken but with sighs? Observe, I beseech you, to what a wretched condition you have reduced me: sad, afflicted, without any possible comfort, unless it proceed from you. Be not then unkind, nor deny, I beg you that little relief which you can only give. Let me have a faithful account of all that concerns you. I would know every thing, be it ever so unfortunate. Perhaps, by mingling my sighs with yours, I may make your sufferings less, if that observation be true, that all sorrows divided are made lighter.

Tell me not, by way of excuse, you will spare our tears; the tears of women, shut up in a melancholy place, and devoted to penitence, are not to be spared. And if you wait for an opportunity to write pleasant and agreeable things to us, you will delay writing too long. Prosperity seldom chuses the side of the virtuous; and Fortune is so blind, that in a crowd in which there is perhaps but one wife and brave man, it is not to be expected she should single him out. Write to me then immediately, and wait not for miracles; they are too scarce, and we too much accustomed to misfortunes to expect any happy turn. I shall always have this, if you please, and this will be always agreeable to me, that when I receive any letters from you, I shall know you still remember me. Seneca, (with whose writings you made me acquainted,) as much a Stoic as he was, seemed to be so very sensible of this kind of pleasure, that upon opening any letters from Lucilius, he imagined he felt the same delight as when they conversed together.

I have made it an observation, since our absence, that we are much fonder of the pictures of those we love, when they are at a great distance, than when they are near to us. It seems to me, as if the farther they are removed their pictures grow the more finished, and acquire a greater resemblance; at least, our imagination, which perpetually figures them to us by the desire we have of seeing them again, makes us think so. By a peculiar power, Love can make that seem life itself, which, as soon as the loved object returns, is nothing but a little canvas and dead colours. I have your picture in my room; I never pass by it without stopping to look at it; and yet when you were present with me, I scarce ever cast my eyes upon it. If a picture, which is but a mute representation of an object, can give such pleasure, what cannot letters inspire? They have souls; they can speak; they have in them all that force which expresses the transports of the heart; they have all the fire of our passions; they can raise them as much as if the persons themselves were present; they have all the softness and delicacy of speech, and sometimes a boldness of expression even beyond it.

We may write to each other; so innocent a pleasure is not forbidden us. Let us not lose, through negligence, the only happiness which is left us, and the only one, perhaps, which the malice of our enemies can never ravish from us. I shall read that you are my husband, and you shall see me address you as a wife. In spite of all your misfortunes, you may be what you please in your letter. Letters were first invented for comforting such solitary wretches as myself. Having lost the substantial pleasures of seeing and possessing you, I shall in some measure compensate this loss by the satisfaction I shall find in your writing. There I shall read your most secret thoughts; I shall carry them always about me; I shall kiss them every moment: if you can be capable of any jealousy, let it be for the fond caresses I shall bestow on your letters, and envy only the happiness of those rivals. That writing may be no trouble to you, write always to me carelessly, and without study: I had rather read the dictates of the heart than of the brain. I cannot live if you do not tell me you always love me; but that language ought to be so natural to you, that I believe you cannot speak otherwise to me without great violence to yourself. And since, by that melancholy relation to your friend, you have awakened all my sorrows, it is but reasonable you should allay them by some marks of an inviolable love.

I do not, however, reproach you for the innocent artifice you made use of to comfort a person in affliction, by comparing his misfortune to another much greater. Charity is ingenious in finding out such pious artifices, and to be commended for using them. But do you owe nothing more to us than to that friend, be the friendship between you ever so intimate? We are called your sisters; we call ourselves your Children; and if it were possible to think of any expression which could signify a dearer relation, or a more affectionate regard and mutual obligation between us, we would use them: if we could be so ungrateful as not to speak our just acknowledgments to you, this church, these altars, these Walls, would reproach our silence, and speak for us, But without leaving it to that, it will be always a pleasure to me to say, that you only are the founder of this house; it is wholly your work. You, by inhabiting here, have given fame and function to a place known before only for robberies and murders. You have, in the literal sense, made the den of thieves a house of prayer. These cloisters owe nothing to public charities; our walls were not raised by the usury of publicans, nor their foundations laid in base extortion. The God whom we serve sees nothing but innocent riches and harmless votaries, whom you have placed here. Whatever this young vineyard is, is owing all to you; and it is your part to employ your whole care to cultivate and improve it; this ought to be one of the principal affairs of your life. Though our holy renunciation, our vows, and our manner of life, seem to secure us from all temptations; though our walls and grates prohibit all approaches, yet it is the outside only, the bark of the tree is covered from injuries; while the sap of original corruption may imperceptibly spread within, even to the heart, and prove fatal to the most promising plantation, unless continual care be taken to cultivate and secure it. Virtue in us is grafted upon Nature and the Woman; the one is weak, and the other is always changeable. To plant the Lord's vine is a work of no little labour; and after it is planted it will require great application and diligence to manure it. The Apostle of the Gentiles; as great a labourer as he was, says, *He hath planted, and Apollo hath watered; but it is God that giveth the increase.* Paul had planted the Gospel among the Corinthians, by his holy and earnest preaching; *Apollos*, a zealous disciple of that great master, continued to cultivate it by frequent exhortations; and the grace of God, which their constant prayers, implored for that church, made the endeavours of both successful.

This ought to be an example for your conduct towards us. I know you are not slothful; yet your labours are not directed to us; your cares are wasted upon a set of men whose thoughts are only earthly, and you refuse to reach out your hand to support those who are weak and staggering in their way to heaven, and who, with all their endeavours, can scarcely preserve themselves from falling. You fling the pearls of the gospel before swine, when you speak to those who are filled with the good things of this world, and nourished with the fatness of the earth; and you neglect the innocent sheep, who, tender as they are, would yet follow you thro' deserts and mountains. Why are such pains thrown away upon the ungrateful, while not a thought is bestowed upon your children, whose souls would be filled with a sense of your goodness? But why should I intreat you in the name of your children? Is it possible I should fear obtaining any thing of you, when I ask it in my own name? And must I use any other prayers than my own to prevail upon you? The St. Austins, Tertullians, and Jeromes, have wrote to the Eudoxas, Paulas, and Melanias; and can you read those names, though of saints, and not remember mine? Can it be criminal for you to imitate St. Jerome, and discourse with me concerning the Scripture? or Tertullian, and preach mortification? or St. Austin, and explain to me the nature of grace? Why should I only reap no advantage from your learning? When you write to me, you will write to your wife. Marriage has made such a correspondence lawful; and since you can, without giving the least scandal, satisfy me, why will you not? I have a barbarous uncle, whose inhumanity is a security against any criminal desire which tenderness and the remembrance of our past enjoyments might inspire. There is nothing that can cause you any fear; you need not fly to conquer. You may see me, hear my sighs, and be a witness of all my sorrows, without incurring any danger, since you can only relieve me with tears and words. If I have put myself into a cloister with reason, persuade me to continue in it with devotion: you have been the occasion of all my misfortunes, you therefore must be the instrument of all my comforts.

You cannot but remember, (for what do not lovers remember?) with what pleasure I have past whole days in hearing your discourse. How, when you were absent, I shut myself from everyone to write to you; how uneasy I was till my letter had come to your hands; what artful management it required to engage confidents. This detail, perhaps, surprises you, and you are in pain for what will fellow. But I am no longer ashamed that my passion has had no bounds for you; for

I have done more than all this: I have hated myself that I might love you; I came hither to ruin myself in a perpetual imprisonment, that I might make you live quiet and easy. Nothing but virtue, joined to a love perfectly disengaged from the commerce of the senses, could have produced such effect. Vice never inspires any thing like this; it is too much enslaved to the body. When we love pleasures, we love the living, and not the dead; we leave off burning with desire for those who can no longer burn for us. This was my cruel uncle's notions; he measured my virtue by the frailty of my sex, and thought it was the man, and not the person, I loved. But he has been guilty to no purpose. I love you more than ever; and to revenge myself of him, I will still love you with all the tenderness of my soul till the last moment of my life. If formerly my affection for you was not so pure, if in those days the mind and the body shared in the pleasure of loving you, I often told you, even then, that I was more pleased with possessing your heart than with any other happiness, and the man was the thing I least valued in you.

You cannot but be entirely persuaded of this by the extreme unwillingness I showed to marry you: tho' I knew that the name of Wife was honourable in the world, and holy in religion, yet the name of your mistress had greater charms, because it was more free. The bonds of matrimony, however honourable, still bear with them a necessary engagement; and I was very unwilling to be necessitated to love always a man who, perhaps, would not always love me. I despised the name of Wife, that I might live happy with that of Mistress; and I find, by your letter to your friend, you have not forgot that delicacy of passion in a woman who loved you always with the utmost tenderness, and yet wished to love you more, you have very justly observed in your letter, that I esteemed those public engagements insipid which form alliances only to be dissolved by death, and which put life and love under the same unhappy necessity. But you have not added how often I have made protestations that it was infinitely preferable to me to live with *Abelard* as his mistress than with any other as empress of the world, and that I was more happy in obeying you, than I should have been in lawfully captivating the lord of the universe. Riches and pomp are not the charms of love. True tenderness make us to separate the lover from all that is external to him, and setting aside his quality, fortune, and employments, consider him singly by himself.

'Tis not love, but the desire of riches and honour, which makes women run into the embraces of an indolent husband. Ambition, not affection, forms such marriages. I believe indeed they may be followed with some honours and advantages, but I can never think that this is the way to enjoy the pleasures of an affectionate union, nor to feel those secret and charming emotions of hearts that have long strove to be united. These martyrs of marriage pine always for large fortunes, which they think they have lost. The wife sees husbands richer that her own, and the husband wives better portioned than his. Their interested vows occasion regret, and regret produces hatred. They soon part, or always desire it. This restless and tormenting passion punishes them for aiming at other advantages of love than love itself.

If there is any thing which may properly be called happiness here below, I am persuaded it is in the union of two persons who love each other with perfect liberty, who are united by a secret inclination, and satisfied with each other's merit; their hearts are full and leave no vacancy for any other passion; they enjoy perpetual tranquillity, because they enjoy content.

If I could believe you as truly persuaded of my merit as I am of yours, I might say there has been such a time when we were such a pair. Alas! how was it possible I should not be certain of your merit? If I could ever have doubted it, the universal esteem would have made me determine in your favour. What country, what city, has not desired your presence? Could you ever retire but you drew the eyes and hearts of all after you? Did not every one rejoice in having seen you? Even women, breaking through the laws of decorum, which custom had imposed upon them, showed manifestly they felt something more for you than esteem. I have known some who have been profuse in their husband's praises, who have yet envied my happiness, and given strong intimations they could have refused you nothing. But what could resist you? Your reputation, which so much soothed the vanity of our sex; your air, your manner; that life in your eyes, which so admirably expressed the vivacity of your mind; your conversation with that ease and elegance which gave every thing you spoke such an agreeable and insinuating turn; in short, every thing spoke for you; very different from some mere scholars, who, with all their learning, have not the capacity to keep up an ordinary conversation, and with all their wit cannot win the affection of women who have a much less share than themselves.

With what ease did you compose verses? and yet those ingenious trifles, which were but a recreation after your more serious studies, are still the entertainment and delight of persons of the best taste. The smallest song, nay, the least sketch of any thing you made for me, had a thousand beauties capable of making it last as long as there are love or lovers in the world. Thus those songs will be sung in honour of other women which you designed only for me? and those tender and natural expressions which spoke your love will help others to explain their passion, with much more advantage than what they themselves are capable of.

What rivals did your gallantries of this kind occasion me? How many ladies laid claim to them? 'Twas a tribute their self-love paid to their beauty. How many have I seen with sighs declare their passion for you, when, after some common visit you had made them, they chanced to be complimented for the Sylvia of your poems? others, in despair and envy, have reproached me, that I had no charms but what your wit bestowed on me, nor in any thing the advantage over them but in being beloved by you. Can you believe if I tell you, that, notwithstanding the vanity of my sex, I thought myself peculiarly happy in having a lover to whom I was obliged for my charms, and took a secret pleasure in being admired by a man who, when he pleased, could raise his mistress to the character of a goddess? Pleased with your glory only, I read with delight all those praises you offered me, and without reflecting how little I deserved, I believed myself such as you described me, that I might be more certain I pleased you.

But oh! where is that happy time fled? I now lament my lover, and of all my joys there remains nothing but the painful remembrance that *they are past.* Now learn, all you my rivals who once viewed my happiness with such jealous eyes, that he you once envied me can never more be yours or mine. I loved him, my love was his crime, and the cause of his punishment. My beauty once charmed him: pleased with each other, we passed our brightest days in tranquillity and happiness. If that was a crime, 'tis a crime I am yet fond of, and I have no other regret, than that against my will I must necessarily be innocent. But what do I say? My misfortune was to have cruel relations, whose malice disturbed the calm we enjoyed. Had they been capable of the returns of reason, I had now been happy in the enjoyment of my dear husband. Oh! how cruel were they when their blind fury urged a villain to surprise you in your sleep! Where was I? Where was your *Heloise* then? What joy should I have had in defending my lover! I would have guarded you from violence, though at the expence of my life; my cries and the shrieks alone would have stopped the hand.—! Oh! whither does the excess of passion hurry me? Here love is shocked, and modesty, joined with despair, deprive me of words. 'Tis eloquence to be silent, where no expression can reach the greatness of the misfortune.

But, tell me, whence proceeds your neglect of me since my being professed? You know nothing moved me to it but your disgrace, nor did I give any consent but yours. Let me hear what is the occasion of your coldness, or give me leave to tell you now my opinion. Was it not the sole view of pleasure which engaged you to me? and has not my tenderness, by leaving you nothing to wish for, extinguished your desires? Wretched *Heloise*! You could please when you wished to avoid it; you merited incense, when you could remove to a distance the hand that offered it; but since your heart has been softened, and has yielded; since you have devoted and sacrificed yourself, you are deserted and forgotten. I am convinced, by sad experience, that it is natural to avoid those to whom we have been too much obliged; and that uncommon generosity produces neglect rather than acknowledgement. My heart surrendered too soon to gain the esteem of the conqueror; you took it without difficulty, and give it up easily. But, ungrateful as you are, I will never content to it. And though in this place I ought not to retain a wish of my own, yet I have ever secretly preserved the desire of being beloved by you. When I pronounced my sad vow, I then had about me your last letter, in which you protested you would be wholly mine, and would never live but to love me. 'Tis to you, therefore, I have offered myself; you had my heart, and I had yours; do not demand any thing back; you must bear with my passion as a thing which of right belongs to you, and from which you can no ways be disengaged.

Alas! what folly is it to talk at this rate? I see nothing here but marks of the Deity, and I speak of nothing but man! You have been the cruel occasion of this by your conduct. Unfaithful man! ought you at once to break off loving me. Why did you not deceive me for a while, rather than immediately abandon me? If you had given me at least but some faint signs even of a dying passion, I myself had favoured the deception. But in vain would I flatter myself that you could be constant; you have left me no colour of making your excuse. I am earnestly desirous to see you; but if that be impossible, I will content myself with a few lines from your hand. Is it so hard for one who loves to write? I ask for none of your letters filled with learning, and writ for reputation; all I desire is such letters as the heart dictates, and which the hand can scarce write fast enough. How did I deceive myself with the hopes that you would be wholly mine when I took the veil, and engaged myself to live for ever under your laws? For in being professed, I vowed no more than to be yours only, and I obliged myself voluntarily to a confinement in which you desired to place me. Death only then can make me leave the place where you have fixed me; and then too, my ashes shall rest, here and wait for your, in order to shew my obedience and devotedness to you to the latest moment possible.

Why should I conceal from you the secret of my call? You know it was neither zeal nor devotion which led me to the cloister. Your conscience is too faithful a witness to permit you to disown it. Yet here I am, and here I will remain; to this place an unfortunate love, and my cruel relations, have condemned me. But if you do not continue your concern for me, If I lose your affection, what have I gained by my imprisonment? What recompense can I hope for? The unhappy consequence of a criminal conduit, and your disgraces, have put on me this habit of chastity, and not the sincere desire of being truly penitent. Thus I strive and labour in vain. Among those whose are wedded to God I serve a man: among the heroic supporters of the Cross, I am a poor slave to a human passion: at the head of a religious community I am devoted to *Abelard* only. What a prodigy am I? Enlighten me, O Lord! Does thy grace or my own despair draw these words from me? I am sensible I am in the Temple of Chastity, covered only with the ashes of that fire which hath consumed us. I am here, I confess, a sinner, but one who, far from weeping for her sins, weeps only for her lover; far from abhorring her crimes, endeavours only to add to them; and who, with a weakness unbecoming the state I am in, please myself continually with the remembrance of past actions, when it is impossible to renew them.

Good God! what is all this! I reproach myself for my own faults, I accuse you for yours, and to what purpose? Veiled as I am, behold in what a disorder you have plunged me! How difficult is it to fight always for duty against inclination? I know what obligations this veil lays on me, but I feel more strongly what power a long habitual passion has over my heart. I am conquered by my inclination. My love troubles my mind, and disorders my will. Sometimes I am swayed by the sentiments of piety which arise in me, and the next moment I yield up my imagination to all that is amorous and tender. I tell you to-day what I would not have said to you yesterday. I had resolved to love you no more; I considered I had made a vow, taken the veil, and am as it were dead and buried; yet there rises unexpectedly from the bottom of my heart a passion which triumphs over all these notions, and darkens all my reason and devotion. You reign in such inward retreats of my soul, that I know not where to attack you. When I endeavour to break those chains by which I am bound to you, I only deceive myself, and all the efforts I am able to make serve but to bind them the faster. Oh, for Pity's sake help a wretch to renounce her desires herself, and if it be possible, even to renounce you! If you are a lover, a father, help a mistress, comfort a child! These tender names, cannot they move you? Yield either to pity or love. If you gratify my request I shall continue a Religious without longer profaning my calling. I am ready to humble myself with you to the wonderful providence of God, who does all things for our sanctification; who, by his grace, pacifies all that is vicious and corrupt in the principle, and; by the inconceivable riches of his mercy, draws us to himself against our wishes, and by degrees opens our eyes to discern the greatness of his bounty, which at first we would not understand.

I thought to end my letter here. But now I am complaining against you, I must unload my heart, and tell you all its jealousies, and reproaches. Indeed I thought it something hard, that when we had both engaged to consecrate ourselves to Heaven, you should insist upon doing it first. Does *Abelard* then, said I, suspect he shall see renewed in me the example of Lot's wife, who could not forbear looking back when she left Sodom? If my youth and sex might give occasion of fear that I should return to the world, could not my behaviour, my fidelity, and this heart which you ought to know, could not banish such ungenerous apprehensions? This distrustful foresight touched me sensibly. I said to myself, there was a time when he could rely upon my bare word, and does he now want vows to secure himself of me? What occasion have I given him in the whole course of my life to admit the least suspicion? I could meet him at all his assignations, and would I decline following him to the feats of holiness? I who have not refused to be a victim of pleasure to gratify him, can he think I would refuse to be a sacrifice of honour to obey him? Has Vice such charms to well-born souls? and, when we have once drank of the cup of sinners, is it with such difficulty that we take the chalice of saints? Or did you believe yourself a greater master to teach vice than virtue, or did you think it was more easy to persuade me to the first than the latter? No, this suspicion would be injurious to both. Virtue is too amiable not to be embraced, when you reveal her charms; and Vice too hideous not to be avoided, when you show her deformities. Nay, when you please, any thing seems lovely to me, and nothing is frightful or difficult when you are by. I am only weak when I am alone and unsupported by you, and therefore it depends on you alone that I may be such as you desire. I wish to Heav'n you had not such a power over me. If you had any occasion to fear, you would be less negligent. But what is there for you to fear? I have done too much, and now have nothing more to do but to triumph over your ingratitude. When we lived happy together, you might have made it doubt whether pleasure or affection united me more to you; but the place from whence I write to you must now have entirely taken away that doubt. Even here I love you as much as ever I did in the world. If I had loved pleasures, could I not yet have found means to have gratified myself? I was not above twenty-two years old; and there were other men left though I was deprived of *Abelard* and yet did I not bury myself alive in a nunnery, and triumph over love, at an age capable of enjoying it in its full latitude? 'Tis to you I sacrifice these remains of a transitory beauty, these widowed nights and tedious days which I pass without seeing you; and since you cannot possess them, I take them from you to offer them to Heaven, and to make, alas! but a secondary oblation of my heart, my days, and my life!

I am sensible I have dwelt too long on this head; I ought to speak less to you of your misfortunes, and of my own sufferings, for love of you. We tarnish the lustre of our most beautiful actions when we applaud them ourselves. This is true, and yet there is a time when we may with decency commend ourselves; when we have to do with those whom base ingratitude has stupefied, we cannot too much praise our own good actions. Now, if you were of this sort of men, this would be a home-reflection on you. Irresolute as I am, I still love you, and yet I must hope for nothing, I have renounced life, and stripped myself of every thing, but I find I neither have nor can renounce my *Abelard*. Though I have lost my lover, I still preserve my love. O vows! O convent! I have not lost my humanity under your inexorable discipline! You have not made me marble by changing my habit. My heart is not totally hardened by my perpetual imprisonment; I am still sensible to what has touched me, though, alas I ought not to be so. Without offending your commands, permit a lover to exhort me to live in obedience to your rigorous rules. Your yoke will be lighter, if that hand support me under it; your exercises will be amiable, if he shows me their advantage. Retirement, solitude! you will not appear terrible, if I may but still know I have any place in his memory. A heart which has been so sensibly affected as mine cannot soon be indifferent. We fluctuate long between love and hatred before we can arrive at a happy tranquillity, and we always flatter ourselves with some distant hope that we shall not be quite forgotten.

Yes, *Abelard*, I conjure you by the chains I bear here to ease the weight of them, and make them as agreeable as I wish they were to me. Teach me the maxims of divine love. Since you have forsaken me, I glory in being wedded to Heaven. My heart adores that title, and disdains any other. Tell me how this divine love is nourished, how it operates, and purifies itself. When we were tossed in the ocean of the world, we could hear of nothing but your verses, which published every where our joys and our pleasures: now we are in the haven of grace, is it not fit that you should discourse to me of this happiness, and teach me every thing which might improve and heighten it? Shew me the same complaisance in my present condition as you did when we were in the world. Without changing the ardour of our affections, let us change their object; let us leave our songs, and sing hymns; let us lift up our hearts to God, and have no transports but for his glory.

I expect this from you as a thing you cannot refuse me. God has a peculiar right over the hearts of great men which he has created. When he pleases to touch them, he ravishes them, and lets them not speak nor breathe but for his glory. Till that moment of grace arrives, O think of me——do not forget me;——remember my love, my fidelity, my constancy; love me as your mistress, cherish me as your child, your sister, your wife. Consider that I still love you, and yet strive to avoid loving you. What a word, what a design is this! I shake with horror, and my heart revolts against what I say. I shall blot all my paper with tears

—I end my long letter, wishing you, if you can desire it, (would to Heaven I could,) for ever adieu.

---

1. *Domino suo, imo Patri; Conjugi suo, imo Fratri; Ancilla sua, imo Filia; ipsius Uxor, imo Soror; Abaelardo Heloisa, &c. Abel. Op.*
2. St. Bernard and St. Norbet.

LETTER III.

ABELARD TO HELOISE.

ADVERTISEMENT.

That the reader may make a right judgment on the following Letter, it is proper he should be informed of the condition *Abelard* was in when he wrote it. The Duke of Britany whose subject he was born, jealous of the glory of France, which then engrossed all the most famous scholars of Europe, and being, besides, acquainted with the persecution *Abelard* had suffered from his enemies, had nominated him to the Abbey of St. Gildas, and, by this benefaction and mark of his esteem, engaged him to past the rest of his days in his dominions. He received this favour with great joy, imagining, that by leaving France he should lose his passion, and gain a new turn of mind upon entering into his new dignity. The Abbey of St. Gildas is seated upon a rock, which the sea beats with its waves. *Abelard*, who had lain on himself the necessity of vanquishing a passion which absence had in a great measure weakened, endeavoured in this solitude to extinguish the remains of it by his tears. But upon his receiving the foregoing letter he could not resist so powerful an attack, but proves as weak and as much to be pitied as *Heloise*. 'Tis not then a master or director that speaks to her, but a man who had loved her, and loves her still: and under this character we are to consider *Abelard* when he wrote the following Letter. If he seems, by some passages in it, to have begun to feel the motions of

divine grace they appear as yet to be only by starts, and without any
uniformity.

～

Could I have imagined that a letter not written to yourself
could have fallen into your hands, I had been more cautious
not to have inserted any thing in it which might awaken the
memory of our past misfortunes. I described with boldness the series
of my disgraces to a friend, in order to make him less sensible of the
loss he had sustained. If by this well meaning artifice I have disturbed
you, I purpose here to dry up those tears which the sad description
occasioned you to shed: I intend to mix my grief with yours, and pour
out my heart before you; in short, to lay open before your eyes all my
trouble, and the secrets of my soul, which my vanity has hitherto made
me conceal from the rest of the world, and which you now force from
me, in spite of my resolutions to the contrary.

It is true, that in a sense of the afflictions which had befallen us,
and observing that no change of our condition was to be expected;
that those prosperous days which had seduced us were now past, and
there remained nothing but to eraze out of our minds, by painful
endeavours, all marks and remembrance of them, I had wished to find
in philosophy and religion a remedy for my disgrace; I searched out an
asylum to secure me from love. I was come to the sad experiment of
making vows to harden my heart. But what have I gained by this? If my
passion has been put under a restraint, my ideas yet remain. I promise
myself that I will forget you, and yet cannot think of it without loving
you; and am pleased with that thought. My love is not at all weakened
by those reflections I make in order to free myself. The silence I am
surrounded with makes me more sensible to its impressions; and while
I am unemployed with any other things, this makes itself the business
of my whole vacation; till, after a multitude of useless endeavours, I
begin to persuade myself that it is a superfluous trouble to drive to free
myself; and that it is wisdom sufficient if I can conceal from every one
but you my confusion and weakness.

I removed to a distance from your person, with an intention of
avoiding you as an enemy; and yet I incessantly seek for you in my
mind; I recall your image in my memory; and in such different disqui-

etudes I betray and contradict myself. I hate you: I love you. Shame presses me on all sides: I am at this moment afraid lest I should seem more indifferent than you, and yet I am ashamed to discover my trouble.

How weak are we in ourselves, if we do not support ourselves on the cross of Christ? Shall we have so little courage, and shall that uncertainty your heart labours with, of serving two masters, affect mine too? You see the confusion I am in, what I blame myself for, and what I suffer. Religion commands me to pursue virtue, since I have nothing to hope for from love. But love still preserves its dominion in my fancy, and entertains itself with past pleasures. Memory supplies the place of a mistress. Piety and duty are not always the fruits of retirement; even in deserts, when the dew of heaven falls not on us, we love what we ought no longer to love. The passions, stirred up by solitude, fill those regions of death and silence; and it is very seldom that what ought to be is truly followed there, and that God only is loved and served. Had I always had such notions as these, I had instructed you better. You call me your Master 'tis true, you were intrusted to my care. I saw you, I was earnest to teach you vain sciences; it cost you your innocence, and me my liberty. Your uncle, who was fond of you, became therefore me enemy, and revenge himself on me. If now, having lost the power of satisfying my passion, I had lost too that of loving you, I should have some consolation. My enemies would have given me that tranquillity which Origen purchased by a crime. How miserable am I! My misfortune does not loose my chains, my passion grows furious by impotence; and that desire I still have for you amidst all my disgraces makes me more unhappy than the misfortune itself. I find myself much more guilty in my thoughts of you, even amidst my tears, than in possessing yourself when I was in full liberty. I continually think of you, I continually call to mind that day when you bestowed on me the first marks of your tenderness. In this condition, O Lord! if I run to prostrate myself before thy altars, if I beseech thee to pity me, why does not the pure flame of thy Spirit consume the sacrifice that is offered to thee? Cannot this habit of penitence which I wear interest Heaven to treat me more favourably? But that is still inexorable; because my passion still lives in me, the fire is only covered over with deceitful ashes, and cannot be extinguished but by extraordinary graces. We deceive men, but nothing is hid from God.

You tell me, that it is for me you live under that veil which covers you; why do you profane your vocation with such words? Why provoke a jealous God by a blasphemy? I hoped, after our separation, you would have changed your sentiments; I hoped too, that God would have delivered me from the tumult of my senses, and that contrariety which reigns in my heart. We commonly die to the affections of those whom we see no more, and they to ours: absence is the tomb of love. But to me absence is an unquiet remembrance of what I once loved, which continually torments me. I flattered myself, that when I should see you no more, you would only rest in my memory, without giving any trouble to my mind; that Britany and the sea would inspire other thoughts; that my fasts and studies would by degrees eraze you out of my heart; but in spite of severe fasts and redoubled studies, in spite of the distance of three hundred miles which separates us, your image, such as you describe yourself in your veil, appears to me, and confounds all my resolutions.

What means have I not used? I have armed my own hands against myself? I have exhausted my strength in constant exercises; I comment upon St. Paul; I dispute with Aristotle; in short, I do all I used to do before I loved you, but all in vain; nothing can be successful that opposes you. Oh! do not add to my miseries by your constancy; forget, if you can, your favours, and that right which they claim over me; permit me to be indifferent. I envy their happiness who have never loved; how quiet and easy are they! But the tide of pleasures has always a reflux of bitterness. I am but too much convinced now of this; but though I am no longer deceived by love, I am not cured: while my reason condemns it, my heart declares for it. I am deplorable that I have not the ability to free myself from a passion which so many circumstances, this place, my person, and my disgraces, tend to destroy. I yield, without considering that a resistance would wipe out my past offences, and would procure me in their stead merit and repose. Why should you use eloquence to reproach me for my flight, and for my silence? Spare the recital of our assignations, and your constant exactness to them; without calling up such disturbing thoughts, I have enough to suffer. What great advantages would philosophy give us over other men, if by studying it we could learn to govern our passions? but how humbled ought we to be when we cannot master them? What efforts, what relapses, what agitations, do we undergo? and how long are we tossed in this confusion, unable to exert our reason, to possess our souls, or to rule our affections?

What a troublesome employment is love! and how valuable is virtue even upon consideration of our own ease! Recoiled your extravagances of passion, guess at my distractions: number up our cares, if possible, our griefs, and our inquietudes; throw these things out of the account, and let love have all its remaining softness and pleasure. How little is that? and, yet for such shadows of enjoyments, which at first appeared to us, are we so weak our whole lives that we cannot now help writing to each other, covered as we are with sackcloth and ashes! How much happier should we be, if, by our humiliation and tears, we could make our repentance sure! The love of pleasure is not eradicated out of the soul but by extraordinary efforts; it has so powerful a party in our breasts, that we find it difficult to condemn it ourselves. What abhorrence can I be said to have of my sins, if the objects of them are always amiable to me? How can I separate from the person I love the passion I must detest? Will the tears I shed be sufficient to render it odious to me? I know not how it happens, there is always a pleasure in weeping for a beloved object. 'Tis difficult in our sorrow to distinguish penitence from love. The memory of the crime, and the memory of the object which has charmed us, are too nearly related to be immediately separated: and the love of God in its beginning does not wholly annihilate the love of the creature. But what excuses could I not find in you, if the crime were excusable? Unprofitable honour, troublesome riches, could never tempt me; but those charms, that beauty, that air, which I yet behold at this instant, have occasioned my fall. Your looks were the beginning of my guilt; your eyes, your discourse, pierced my heart; and in spite of that ambition and glory which filled it, and offered to make defence, love soon made itself master. God, in order to punish me, forsook me. His providence permitted those consequences which have since happened. You are no longer of the world; you have renounced it; I am a Religious, devoted to solitude; shall we make no advantage of our condition? Would you destroy my piety in its infant-state? Would you have me forsake the convent into which I am but newly entered? Must I renounce my vows? I have made them in the presence of God; whither shall I fly from his wrath if I violate them? Suffer me to seek for ease in my duty; how difficult it is to procure that! I pass whole days and nights alone in this cloister, without closing

my eyes. My love burns fiercer, amidst the happy indifference of those
who surround me, and my heart is at once pierced with your sorrows
and its own. Oh what a loss have I sustained, when I consider your
constancy! What pleasures have I missed enjoying! I ought not to
confess this weakness to you: I am sensible I commit a fault: if I could
have showed more firmness of mind, I should, perhaps, have provoked
your resentment against me, and your anger might work that effect in
you which your virtue could not. If in the world I published my weakness by verses and love-songs, ought not the dark cells of this house to
conceal that weakness, at least, under an appearance of piety? Alas! I
am still the same! or if I avoid the evil, I cannot do the good; and yet I
ought to join both, in order to make this manner of living profitable.
But how difficult is this in the trouble which surrounds me? Duty,
reason, and decency, which, upon other occasions have such power
over me, are here entirely useless. The gospel is a language I do not
understand, when it opposes my passion. Those oaths which I have
taken before the holy altar, are feeble helps when opposed to you.
Amidst so many voices which call me to my duty, I hear and obey
nothing but the secret dictates of a desperate passion. Void of all relish
for virtue, any concern for my condition, or any application to my
studies, I am continually present by my imagination where I ought not
to be, and I find I have no power, when I would at any time correct it.
I feel a perpetual strife between my inclination and my duty. I find
myself entirely a distracted lover; unquiet in the midst of silence, and
restless in this abode of peace and repose. How shameful is such a
condition!

Consider me no more, I intreat you, as a founder, or any great
personage; your encomiums do but ill agree with such multiplied weaknesses. I am a miserable sinner, prostrate before my Judge, and, with
my face pressed to the earth, I mix my tears and my sighs in the dust,
when the beams of grace and reason enlighten me. Come, see me in
this posture, and solicit me to love you! Come, if you think fit, and in
your holy habit thrust yourself between God and me and be a wall of
separation! Come, and force from me those sighs, thoughts, and vows,
which I owe to him only. Assist the evil spirits, and be the instrument
of their malice. What cannot you induce a heart to, whose weakness
you so perfectly know? But rather withdraw yourself, and contribute to
my salvation. Suffer me to avoid destruction, I intreat you, by our

former tenderest affection, and by our common misfortune. It will always be the highest love to show none. I here release you of all your oaths and engagements. Be God's wholly, to whom you are appropriated; I will never oppose so pious a design. How happy shall I be if I thus lose you! then shall I be indeed a Religious, and you a perfect example of an Abbess.

Make yourself amends by so glorious a choice; make your virtue a spectacle worthy men and angels: be humble among your children, assiduous in your choir, exact in your discipline, diligent in your reading; make even your recreations useful. Have you purchased your vocation at so slight a rate, as that you should not turn it to the best advantage? Since you have permitted yourself to be abused by false doctrine, and criminal instructions, resist not those good-counsels which grace and religion inspire me with. I will confess to you, I have thought myself hitherto an abler master to instill vice than to excite virtue, My false eloquence has only set off false good. My heart drunk with voluptuousness, could only suggest terms proper and moving to recommend that. The cup of sinners overflows with so inchanting a sweetness and we are naturally so much inclined to taste it, that it needs only be offered to us. On the other hand, the chalice of saints is filled with a bitter draught, and nature starts from it. And yet you reproach me with cowardice for giving it you first; I willingly submit to these accusations. I cannot enough admire the readiness you showed to take the religious habit: bear, therefore, with courage the Cross, which you have taken up so resolutely. Drink of the chalice of saints, even to the bottom, without turning your eyes with uncertainty upon me, Let me remove far from you, and obey the apostle, who hath said, *Fly*.

You intreat me to return, under a pretence of devotion, Your earnestness in this point creates a suspicion in me, and makes me doubtful how to answer you. Should I commit an error here, my words would blush, if I may say so, after the history of my misfortunes. The Church is jealous of its glory, and commands that her children should be induced to the practice of virtue by virtuous means. When we have approached God after an unblameable manner, we may then with boldness invite others to him. But to forget *Heloise*, to see her no more, is what Heaven demands of *Abelard*; and to expect nothing from *Abelard*, to lose him even in idea, is what Heaven enjoins *Heloise*. To forget in the case of love is the most necessary penitence, and the most difficult. It is easy to recount our faults. How many through indiscretion have made themselves a second pleasure of this, instead of confessing them with humility. The only way to return to God is, by neglecting the creature which we have adored, and adoring God whom we have neglected. This may appear harsh, but it must be done if we would be saved.

To make it more easy, observe why I pressed you to your vow before I took mine; and pardon my sincerity, and the design I have of meriting your neglect and hatred, if I conceal nothing from you of the particular you inquire after. When I saw myself so oppressed with my misfortune, my impotency made me jealous, and I considered all men as my rivals. Love has more of distrust than assurance. I was apprehensive of abundance of things, because I saw I had abundance of defects; and being tormented with fear from my own example, I imagined your heart, which had been so much accustomed to love, would not be long without entering into a new engagement. Jealousy can easily believe to most dreadful consequences, I was desirous to put myself out of a possibility of doubting you. I was very urgent to persuade you, that decency required you should withdraw from the envious eyes of the world; that modesty, and our friendship, demanded it; nay, that your own safety obliged you to it; and, that after such a revenge taken upon me, you could expect to be secure no where but in a convent.

I will do you justice; you were very easily persuaded to it. My jealousy secretly triumphed over your innocent compliance; and yet, triumphant as I was, I yielded you up to God with an unwilling heart. I still kept my gift as much as was possible, and only parted with it that I might effectually put it out of the power of men. I did not persuade you to religion out of any regard to your happiness, but condemned you to it, like an enemy who destroys what he cannot carry off. And yet you heard my discourses with kindness; you sometimes interrupted me with tears, and pressed me to acquaint you which of the convents was most in my esteem. What a comfort did I feel in seeing you shut up! I was now at ease, and took a satisfaction in considering that you did not continue long in the world after my disgrace, and that you would return into it no more.

But still this was doubtful. I imagined women were incapable of maintaining any constant resolutions, unless they were forced by the necessity of fixed vows. I wanted those vows, and Heaven itself, for your security, that I might no longer distrust you. Ye holy mansions, ye impenetrable retreats, from what numberless apprehensions have you freed me? Religion and Piety keep a strict guard round your grates and high walls. What a haven of rest is this to a jealous mind? and with what impatience did I endeavour it! I went every day trembling to exhort you to this sacrifice; I admired, without daring to mention it then, a brightness in your beauty which I had never observed before. Whether it was the bloom of a rising virtue, or an anticipation of that great loss I was going to suffer, I was not curious in examining the cause, but only hastened your being professed. I engaged your Prioress in my guilt by a criminal bribe, with which I purchased the right of burying you. The professed of the house were also bribed, and concealed from you, by my directions, all their scruples and disgusts. I omitted nothing, either little or great: and if you had escaped all my snares, I myself would not have retired: I was resolved to follow you every where. This shadow of myself would always have pursued your steps, and continually occasioned either your confusion or fear, which would have been a sensible gratification to me.

But, thanks to Heaven, you resolved to make a vow; I accompanied you with terror to the foot of the altar: and while you stretched out your hand to touch the sacred cloth, I heard you pronounce distinctly those fatal words which for ever separated you from all men. 'Till then your beauty and youth seemed to oppose my design, and to threaten your return into the world. Might not a small temptation have changed you? Is it possible to renounce one's self entirely at the age of two and twenty? at an age which claims the most absolute liberty, could you think the world no longer worthy of your regard? How much did I wrong you, and what weakness did I impute to you? You were in my imagination nothing but lightness and inconstancy. Might not a young woman, at the noise of the flames, and the fall of Sodom, look back, and pity some one person? I took notice of your eyes, your motion, your air; I trembled at every thing. You may call such a self-interested conduct treachery, perfidiousness, murder. A love which was so like to hatred ought to provoke the utmost contempt and anger.

It is fit you should know, that the very moment when I was convinced of your being entirely devoted to me, when I saw you were infinitely worthy of all my love and acknowledgement, I imagined I could love you no more; I thought it time to leave off giving you any marks of affection; and I considered, that by your holy espousals you were now the peculiar care of Heaven, even in the quality of a wife. My jealousy seemed to be extinguished. When God only is our rival, we have nothing to fear: and being in greater tranquillity than ever before, I dared even to offer up prayers, and beseech him to take you away from my eyes: but it was not a time to make rash prayers; and my faith was too imperfect to let them be heard. He who sees the depth and secrets of all men's hearts, saw mine did not agree with my words. Necessity and despair were the springs of this proceeding. Thus I inadvertently offered an insult to Heaven rather than a sacrifice. God rejected my offering and my prayers, and continued my punishment, by suffering me to continue my love. Thus, under the guilt of your vows, and of the passion which preceded them, I must be tormented all the days of my life.

If God spoke to your heart, as to that of a Religious, whose innocence had first engaged him to heap on it a thousand favours, I should have matter of comfort; but to see both of us victims of a criminal love; to see this love insult us, and invest itself with our very habits, as with spoils it has taken from our devotion, fills me with horror and trembling. Is this a state of reprobation? or are these the consequences of a long drunkenness in profane love? We cannot say love is a drunkenness and a poison till we are illuminated by grace; in the mean time, it is an evil which we dote on. When we are under such a mistake the knowledge of our misery is the first step towards amendment. Who does not know that it is for the glory of God to find no other foundation in man for his mercy than man's very weakness? When he has shewed us this weakness, and we bewail it, he is ready to put forth his omnipotence to assist us. Let us say for our comfort that what we suffer is one of those long and terrible temptations which have sometimes disturbed the vocations of the most Holy.

God can afford his presence to men, in order to soften their calamities, whenever he shall think fit. It was his pleasure when you took the veil, to draw you to him by his grace. I saw your eyes, when you spoke your last farewell, fixed upon the cross. It was above six months before you wrote me a letter, nor during all that time did I receive any message from you. I admired this silence, which I durst not blame, and could not imitate. I wrote to you; you returned me no answer. Your heart was then shut; but this guardian of the spouse is now opened, he is withdrawn from it, and has left you alone. By removing from you, he has made trial of you; call him back and strive to regain him. We must have the assistance of God that we may break our chains; we have engaged too deeply in love to free ourselves. Our follies have penetrated even into the most sacred places. Our amours have been matter of scandal to a whole kingdom. They are read and admired; love which produced them has caused them to be described. We shall be a consolation for the failings of youth hereafter. Those who offend after us will think themselves less guilty. We are criminals whose repentance is late. O may it be sincere! Let us repair, as far is possible, the evils we have done; and let France, which has been the witness of our crimes, be astonished at our penitence. Let us confound all who would imitate our guilt, let us take the part of God against ourselves, and by so doing prevent his judgment. Our former irregularities require tears, shame, and sorrow to expiate them. Let us offer up these sacrifices from our hearts; let us blush, let us weep. If in these weak beginnings, Lord, our heart is not entirely thine, let it at least be made sensible that it ought to be so!

Deliver yourself, *Heloise*, from the shameful remains of a passion which has taken too deep root. Remember that the least thought for any other than God is adultery. If you could see me here, with my meagre face and melancholy air, surrounded with numbers of persecuting monks, who are alarmed at my reputation for learning, and offended at my lean visage, as if I threatened them with a reformation; what would you say of my base sighs, and of those unprofitable tears which deceive these credulous men? Alas! I am humbled under love, and not under the Cross. Pity me, and free yourself. If your vocation be, as you say, my work, deprive me not of the merit of it by your continual inquietudes. Tell me that you, will honour the habit which covers you, by an inward retirement. Fear God, that you may be delivered from your frailties. Love him, if you would advance in virtue. Be not uneasy in the cloister, for it is the dwelling of saints. Embrace your bands, they are the chains of Christ Jesus: he will lighten them, and bear them with you, if you bear them with humility.

Without growing severe to a passion which yet possesses you, learn from your own misery to succour your weak sisters; pity them upon consideration of your own faults. And if any thoughts too natural shall importune you, fly to the foot of the Cross, and beg for mercy; there are wounds open; lament before the dying Deity. At the head of a religious society be not a slave, and having rule over queens, begin to govern yourself. Blush at the least revolt of your senses. Remember, that even at the foot of the altar we often sacrifice to lying spirits, and that no incense can be more agreeable to them than that which in those places burns in the heart of a Religious still sensible of passion and love. If, during your abode in the world, your soul has acquired a habit of loving, feel it now no more but for Jesus Christ, Repent of all the moments of your life which you have wasted upon the world, and upon pleasure; demand them of me, it is a robbery which I am guilty of; take courage and boldly reproach me with it.

I have been indeed your master, but it was only to teach you sin. You call me your Father; before I had any claim to this title I deserved that of Parricide. I am your brother, but it is the affinity of our crimes that has purchased me that distinction. I am called your Husband, but it is after a public scandal. If you have abused the sanctity of so many venerable names in the superscription of your letters, to do me honour, and flatter your own passion, blot them out, and place in their stead those of a Murtherer, a Villain, an Enemy, who has conspired against your honour, troubled your quiet, and betrayed your innocence. You would have perished thro' my means, but by an extraordinary act of grace, which that you might be saved, has thrown me down in the middle of my course.

This is the idea that you ought to have of a fugitive, who endeavours to deprive you of the hope of seeing him any more. But when love has once been sincere, how difficult it is to determine to love no more? 'Tis a thousand times more easy to renounce the world than love. I hate this deceitful faithless world; I think no more of it; but my heart, still wandering, will eternally make me feel the anguish of having lost you, in spite of all the convictions of my understanding. In the mean time tho' I so be so cowardly as to retract what you have read, do not suffer me to offer myself to your thoughts but under this last notion. Remember my last endeavours were to seduce your heart. You perished by my means, and I with you. The same waves swallowed us both up. We waited for death with indifference, and the same death had carried us headlong to the same punishments. But Providence has turned off this blow, and our shipwreck has thrown us into an haven.

There are some whom the mercy of God saves by afflictions. Let my salvation be the fruit of your prayers! let me owe it to your tears, or exemplary holiness! Tho' my heart, Lord! be filled with the love of one of thy creatures, thy hand can, when it pleases, draw out of it those ideas which fill its whole capacity. To love *Heloise* truly is to leave her entirely to that quiet which retirement and virtue afford. I have resolved it: this letter shall be my last fault. Adieu.

If I die here, I will give orders that my body be carried to the house of the Paraclete. You shall see me in that condition; not to demand tears from you, it will then be too late; weep rather for me now, to extinguish that fire which burns me. You shall see me, to strengthen your piety by the horror of this carcase; and my death, then more eloquent than I can be, will tell you what you love when you love a man. I hope you will be contented, when you have finished this mortal life, to be buried near me. Your cold ashes need then fear nothing, and my tomb will, by that means, be more rich and more renowned.

LETTER IV.

HELOISE TO ABELARD.

In the following Letter the passion of *Heloise* breaks, out with more violence than ever. That which she had received from *Abelard*, instead of fortifying her resolutions, served only to revive in her memory all their past endearments and misfortunes. With this impression she writes again to her husband; and appears now, not so much in the charter of a Religious, striving with the remains of her former weakness, as in that of an unhappy woman abandoned to all the transport of love and despair.

To *Abelard*, her well beloved in Christ Jesus, from *Heloise*, his well-beloved, in the same Christ Jesus.

I read the letter I received from you with abundance of impatience. In spite of all my misfortunes, I hoped to find nothing in it besides arguments of comfort; but how ingenious are lovers in tormenting themselves! Judge of the exquisite sensibility and force of my love by that which causes the grief of my soul; I was disturbed at the superscription of your letter! why did you place the name of *Heloise* before that of *Abelard*? what means this most cruel and unjust distinction? 'Twas your name only, the name of Father, and of a

Husband, which my eager eyes sought after. I did not look for my own, which I much rather, if possible, forget, as being the cause of your misfortune. The rules of decorum, and the character of Master and Director which you have over me, opposed that ceremonious manner of addressing me; and Love commanded you to banish it. Alas! you know all this but too well.

Did you write thus to me before Fortune had ruined my happiness? I see your heart has deserted me, and you have made greater advances in the way of devotion than I could wish. Alas! I am too weak to follow you; condescend at least to stay for me, and animate me with your advice. Will you have the cruelty to abandon me? The fear of this stabs my heart: but the fearful presages you make at the latter end of your Letter, those terrible images you draw of your death, quite distracts me. Cruel *Abelard*! you ought to have stopped my tears, and you make them flow; you ought to have quieted the disorder of my heart, and you throw me into despair.

You desire that after your death I should take care of your ashes, and pay them the last duties. Alas! in what temper did you conceive these mournful ideas? and how could you describe them to me? Did not the apprehension of causing my present death make the pen drop from your hand? You did not reflect, I suppose, upon all those' torments to which you were going to deliver me. Heaven, as severe as it has been against me, is not in so great a degree so, as to permit me to live one moment after you. Life without my *Abelard* is an unsupportable punishment, and death a most exquisite happiness, if by that means I can be united with him. If Heaven hears the prayers I continually make for you, your days will be prolonged, and you will bury me.

Is it not your part to prepare me, by your powerful exhortations against that great crisis, which shakes the most resolute and confirmed minds? Is it not your part to receive my last sighs; take care of my funeral, and give an account of my manners and faith? Who but you can recommend us worthily to God; and by the fervour and merit of your prayers, conduct those souls to him which you have joined to his worship by solemn contracts? We expect these pious offices from your paternal charity. After this you will be free from those disquietudes which now molest you, and you will quit life with more ease, whenever it shall please God to call you away. You may follow us, content with what you have done, and in a full assurance of our happiness: but till then, write not to me any such terrible things. Are we not already sufficiently miserable? must we aggravate our sorrows? Our life here is but a languishing death? will you hasten it? Our present disgraces are sufficient to employ our thoughts continually, and shall we seek new arguments of grief in futurities? How void of reason are men, said Seneca, to make distant evils present by reflection, and to take pains before death to lose all the comforts of life?

When you have finished your course here below, you say it is your desire that your body be carried to the house of the Paraclete, to the intent that, being always exposed to my eyes, you may be for ever present to my mind; and that your dear body may strengthen our piety, and animate our prayers. Can you think that the traces you have drawn in my heart can ever be worn out? or that any length of time can obliterate the memory we have here of your benefits? And what time shall I find for those prayers you speak of? Alas! I shall then be filled with other cares. Can so heavy a misfortune leave me a moment's quiet? can my feeble reason resist such powerful assaults? When I am distracted and raving, (if I dare to say it,) even against Heaven itself, I shall not soften it by my prayers, but rather provoke it by my cries and reproaches! But how should I pray! or how bear up against my grief? I should be more urgent to follow you than to pay you the sad ceremonies of burial. It is for you for *Abelard*, that I have resolved to live; if you are ravished from me, what use can I make of my miserable days? Alas! what lamentations should I make, if Heaven, by a cruel pity, should preserve me till that moment? When I but think of this last separation; I feel all the pangs of death; what shall I be then, if I should see this dreadful hour? Forbear, therefore, to infuse into my mind such mournful thoughts, if not for love, at least for pity.

You desire me to give myself up to my duty, and to be wholly God's, to whom I am consecrated. How can I do that when you frighten me with apprehensions that continually possess my mind day and night? When an evil threatens us, and it is impossible to ward it off, why do we give up ourselves to the unprofitable fear of it, which is yet even more tormenting than the evil itself?

What have I to hope for after this loss of you? what can confine me to earth when Death shall have taken away from me all that was dear upon it? I have renounced without difficulty all the charms of life, preserving only my love, and the secret pleasure of thinking incessantly of you, and hearing that you live; and yet alas! you do not live for me, and I dare not even flatter myself with the hopes that I shall ever enjoy a sight of you more. This is the greatest of my afflictions. Merciless Fortune! hast thou not persecuted me enough? Thou dost not give me any respite? thou hast exhausted all thy vengeance upon me, and reserved thyself nothing whereby thou mayst appear terrible to others. Thou hast wearied thyself in tormenting me, and others have nothing now to fear from thy anger. But to what purpose dost thou still arm thyself against me? The wounds I have already received leave no room for new ones; why cannot I urge thee to kill me? or dost thou fear, amidst the numerous torments thou heapest on me, dost thou fear that such a stroke would deliver me from all? Therefore thou preservest me from death, in order to make me die every moment.

Dear *Abelard*, pity my despair! Was ever any thing so miserable! The higher you raised me above other women who envied me your love, the more sensible am I now of the loss of your heart. I was exalted to the top of happiness, only that I might have a more terrible fall. Nothing could formerly be compared to my pleasures, and nothing now can equal my misery. My glory once raised the envy of my rivals; my present wretchedness moves the compassion of all that see me. My fortune has been always in extremes, she has heaped on me her most delightful favours, that she might load me with the greatest of her afflictions. Ingenious in tormenting me, she has made the memory of the joys I have lost, an inexhaustible spring of my tears. Love, which possest was her greatest gift, being taken away, occasions all my sorrow. In short, her malice has entirely succeeded, and I find my present afflictions proportionably bitter as the transports which charmed me were sweet.

But what aggravates my sufferings yet more, is, that we began to be miserable at a time when we seemed the least to deserve it. While we gave ourselves up to the enjoyment of a criminal love, nothing opposed our vicious pleasures. But scarce had we retrenched what was unlawful in our passion, and taken refuge in marriage against that remorse which might have pursued us, but the whole wrath of heaven fell on us in all its weight. But how barbarous was your punishment? The very remembrance makes me shake with horror. Could an outrageous husband make a villain suffer more that had dishonoured his bed? Ah! What right had a cruel uncle over us? We were joined to each other even before the altar, which should have protected you from the rage of your enemies. Must a wife draw on you that punishment which ought not to fall on any but an adulterous lover? Besides, we were separated; you were busy in your exercises, and instructed a learned auditory in mysteries which the greatest geniuses before you were not able to penetrate; and I, in obedience to you, retired to a cloister. I there spent whole days in thinking of you, and sometimes meditating on holy lessons, to which I endeavoured to apply myself. In this very juncture you became the victim of the most unhappy love. You alone expiated the crime common to us both: You only were punished, though both of us were guilty. You, who were least so, was the object of the whole vengeance of a barbarous man. But why should I rave at your assassins? I, wretched I, have ruined you, I have been the original of all your misfortunes! Good Heaven! Why was I born to be the occasion of so tragical an accident? How dangerous is it for a great man to suffer himself to be moved by our sex! He ought from his infancy to be inured to insensibility of heart, against all our charms. *Hearken, my Son*, (said formerly the wisest of Men) *attend and keep my instructions; if a beautiful woman by her looks endeavour to intice thee, permit not thyself to be overcome by a corrupt inclination; reject the poison she offers, and follow not the paths which she directs. Her house is the gate of destruction and death*. I have long examined things, and have found that death itself is a less dangerous evil than beauty. 'Tis the shipwreck of liberty, a fatal snare, from which it is impossible ever to get free. 'Twas woman which threw down the first man from that glorious condition in which heaven had placed him. She who was created in order to partake of his happiness, was the sole cause of his ruin. How bright had been the glory, *Sampson*, if thy heart had been as firm against the charms of *Dalilah*, as against the weapons of the *Philistines*! A woman disarmed and betrayed thee, who hadst been a glorious conqueror of armies. Thou saw'st thyself delivered into the hands of they enemies; thou wast deprived of thy eyes, those inlets of love into thy soul: distracted and despairing didst thou die, without any consolation but that of involving thy enemies in thy destruction. *Solomon*, that he might please women, forsook the care of pleasing God. That king, whose wisdom princes came from all parts to admire, he whom God had chose to build him a temple, abandoned the worship of those very alters he had had defended, and proceeded to such a pitch of folly as even to burn incense to idols. *Job* had no enemy more cruel than his wife: what temptations did he not bear? The evil spirit, who had declared himself his persecutor, employed a woman as an instrument to shake his constancy; and the same evil spirit made *Heloise* an instrument to ruin *Abelard!* All the poor comfort I have is, that I am not the voluntary cause of your misfortune. I have not betrayed you; but my constancy and love have been destructive to you. If I have committed a crime in having loved you with constancy, I shall never be able to repent of that crime. Indeed I gave myself up too much to the captivity of those soft errors into which my rising passion seduced me. I have endeavoured to please you even at the expence of my virtue, and therefore deserve those pains I feel. My guilty transports could not but have a tragical end. As soon as I was persuaded of your love, alas! I scarce delayed a moment, resigning myself to all your protestations. To be beloved by *Abelard* was, in my esteem, too much glory, and I too impatiently desired it not to believe it immediately. I endeavoured at nothing but convincing you of my utmost passion. I made no use of those defences of disdain and honour; those enemies of pleasure which tyrannize over our sex, made in me but a weak and unprofitable resistance. I sacrificed all to my love, and I forced my duty to give place to the ambition of making happy the most gallant and learned person of the age. If any consideration had been able to stop me, it would have been without doubt the interest of my love. I feared, lest having nothing further for you to desire, your passion might become languid, and you might seek for new pleasures in some new conquest. But it was easy for you to cure me of a suspicion so opposite to my own inclination. I ought to have forseen other more certain evils, and to have considered, that the idea of lost enjoyments would be the trouble of my whole life.

How happy should I be could I wash out with my tears the memory of those pleasures which yet I think of with delight? At least I will exert some generous endeavour, and, by smothering in my heart those desires to which the frailty of my nature may give birth, I will exercise torments upon myself, like those the rage of your enemies has made you suffer. I will endeavour by that means to satisfy you at least, if I cannot appease an angry God. For, to show you what a deplorable condition I am in, and how far my repentance is from being available, I dare even accuse Heaven every moment of cruelty for delivering you into those snares which were prepared for you. My repinings kindle the divine wrath, when I should endeavour to draw down mercy.

In order to expiate a crime, it is not sufficient that we bear the punishment; whatever we suffer is accounted as nothing, if the passions still continue, and the heart is inflamed with the same desires. It is an easy matter to confess a weakness, and to inflict some punishment upon ourselves; but it is the last violence to our nature to extinguish the memory of pleasures which, by a sweet habit, have gained absolute possession of our minds. How many persons do we observe who make an outward confession of their faults, yet, far from being afflicted for them, take a new pleasure in the relating them. Bitterness of heart ought to accompany the confession of the mouth, yet that very rarely happens. I, who have experienced so many pleasures in loving you, feel, in spite of myself that I cannot repent of them, nor forbear enjoying them over again as much as is possible, by recollecting them in my memory. Whatever endeavours I use, on whatever side I turn me, the sweet idea still pursues me and every object brings to my mind what I ought to forget. During the still night, when my heart ought to be in quiet in the midst of sleep, which suspends the greatest disturbances, I cannot avoid those illusions my heart entertains. I think I am still with my dear *Abelard*. I see him, I speak to him, and hear him answer. Charmed with each other, we quit our philosophic studies to entertain ourselves with our passion. Sometimes, too, I seem to be a witness of the bloody enterprise of your enemies; I oppose their fury; I fill our apartment with fearful cries, and in a moment I wake in tears. Even in holy places before the altar I carry with me the memory of our guilty loves. They are my whole business, and, far from lamenting for having been seduced, I sigh for having lost them.

I remember (for nothing is forgot by lovers) the time and place in which you first declared your love to me, and swore you would love me till death. Your words, your oaths, are all deeply graven in my heart. The disorder of my discourse discovers to everyone the trouble of my mind. My sighs betray me; and your name is continually in my mouth. When I am in this condition, why dost not thou, O Lord, pity my weakness, and strengthen me by thy grace? You are happy, *Abelard*; this grace has prevented you; and your misfortune has been the occasion of your finding rest. The punishment of your body has cured the deadly wounds of your soul. The tempest has driven you into the haven. God who seemed to lay his hand heavily upon you, fought only to help you: he is a father chastising, and not an enemy revenging; a wife physician, putting you to some pain in order to preserve your life. I am a thousand times more to be lamented than you; I have a thousand passions to combat with. I must resist those fires which Jove kindles in a young heart. Our sex is nothing but weakness, and I have the greater difficulty to defend myself, because the enemy that attacks me pleases. I dote on the danger which threatens me, how then can I avoid falling?

In the midst of these struggles I endeavour at least to conceal my weakness from those you have entrusted to my care. All who are about me admired my virtue, but could their eyes penetrate into my heart, what would they not discover? My passions there are in a rebellion; I preside over others, but cannot rule myself. I have but a false covering, and this seeming virtue is a real vice. Men judge me praise-worthy, but I am guilty before God, from whose all-seeing eye nothing is hid, and who views, through all their foldings, the secrets of all hearts. I cannot escape his discovery. And yet it is a great deal to me to maintain even this appearance of virtue. This troublesome hypocrisy is in some sort commendable. I give no scandal to the world, which is so easy to take bad impressions. I do not shake the virtue of these feeble ones who are under my conduct. With my heart full of the love of man, I exhort them at least to love only God: charmed with the pomp of worldly pleasures, I endeavour to show them that they are all deceit and vanity. I have just strength enough to conceal from them my inclinations, and I look upon that as a powerful effect of grace. If it is not sufficient to make me embrace virtue, it is enough to keep me from committing sin.

And yet it is in vain to endeavour to separate those two things. They must be guilty who merit nothing; and they depart from virtue who delay to approach it. Besides, we ought to have no other motive than the love of God. Alas! what can I then hope for? I own, to my confusion, I fear more the offending of man than the provoking of God, and study less to please him than you. Yes, it was your command only, and not a sincere vocation, as is imagined, that shut me up in these cloisters. I fought to give you ease, and not to sanctify myself. How unhappy am I? I tear myself from all that pleases me? I bury myself here alive, I exercise my self in the most rigid fastings; and such severities as cruel laws impose on us; I feed myself with tears and sorrows, and, notwithstanding this, I deserve nothing for all the hardships I suffer. My false piety has long deceived you as well as others. You have thought me easy, and yet I was more disturbed than ever. You persuaded yourself I was wholly taken up with my duty, yet I had no business but love. Under this mistake you desire my prayers; alas! I must expect yours. Do not presume upon my virtue and my care. I am wavering, and you must fix me by your advice. I am yet feeble, you must sustain and guide me by your counsel.

What occasion had you to praise me? praise is often hurtful to those on whom it is bestowed. A secret vanity springs up in the heart, blinds us, and conceals from us wounds that are ill cured. A seducer flatters us, and at the same time, aims at our destruction. A sincere friend disguises nothing from us, and from passing a light hand over the wound, makes us feel it the more intensely, by applying remedies. Why do you not deal after this manner with me? Will you be esteemed a base dangerous flatterer; or, if you chance to see any thing commendable in me, have you no fear that vanity, which is so natural to all women, should quite efface it? but let us not judge of virtue by outward appearances, for then the reprobates as well as the elect may lay claim to it. An artful impostor may, by his address gain more admiration than the true zeal of a saint.

The heart of man is a labyrinth, whose windings are very difficult to be discovered. The praises you give me are the more dangerous, in regard that I love the person who gives them. The more I desire to please you, the readier am I to believe all the merit you attribute to me. Ah, think rather how to support my weaknesses by wholesome remonstrances! Be rather fearful than confident of my salvation: say our virtue is founded upon weakness, and that those only will be crowned who have fought with the greatest difficulties: but I seek not for that crown which is the reward of victory, I am content to avoid only the danger. It is easier to keep off than to win a battle. There are several degrees in glory, and I am not ambitious of the highest; those I leave to souls of great courage, who have been often victorious. I seek not to conquer, out of fear lest I should be overcome. Happy enough, if I can escape shipwreck, and at last gain the port. Heaven commands me to renounce that fatal passion which unites me to you; but oh! my heart will never be able to consent to it. Adieu.

LETTER V.

HELOISE TO ABELARD.

Heloise had been dangerously ill at the Convent of the Paraclete: immediately upon her recovery she wrote this Letter to *Abelard*, She seems now to have disengaged herself from him, and to have resolved to think of nothing but repentance; yet discovers some emotions, which make it doubtful whether devotion had entirely triumphed over her passion.

Dear *Abelard*, you expect, perhaps, that I should accuse you of negligence. You have not answered my last letter; and thanks to Heaven, in the condition I now am, it is a happiness to me that you show so much insensibility for the fatal passion which had engaged me to you. At last *Abelard*, you have lost *Heloise* for ever. Notwithstanding all the oaths I made to think of nothing but you only, and to be entertained with nothing but you, I have banished you from my thoughts, I have forgot you. Thou charming idea of a lover I once adored, thou wilt no more be my happiness! Dear image of *Abelard*! thou wilt no more follow me every where; I will no more remember thee. O celebrated merit of a man, who, in spite of his enemies is the wonder of his age! O enchanting pleasures, to which *Heloise* entirely resigned herself, you, you have been my tormentors! I confess *Abelard*, without a blush, my infidelity; let my inconstancy teach the world that there is no depending upon the promises of women; they are all subject to change. This troubles you, *Abelard*; this news, without doubt, surprises you; you could never imagine *Heloise*, should be inconstant. She was prejudiced by so strong an inclination to you, that you cannot conceive how time could alter it. But be undeceived; I am going to discover to you my falseness, though instead of reproaching me, I persuade myself you will shed tears of joy. When I shall have told you what rival hath ravished my heart from you, you will praise my inconstancy, and will pray this rival to fix it. By this you may judge that it is God alone that takes *Heloise* from you. Yes, my dear *Abelard*, he gives my mind that tranquillity which a quick remembrance of our misfortunes would not suffer me to enjoy. Just Heaven! what other rival could take me from you? Could you imagine it possible for any mortal to blot you from my heart? Could you think me guilty of sacrificing the virtuous and learned *Abelard* to any other but to God? No, I believe you have done me justice in this point. I question not but you are impatient to know what means God used to accomplish so great an end; I will tell you, and wonder at the secret ways of Providence. Some few days after you sent me your last letter I fell dangerously ill; the physicians gave me over; and I expected certain death. Then it was that my passion, which always before seemed innocent, appeared criminal to me. My memory represented faithfully to me all the past actions of my life, and I confess to you my love was the only pain I felt. Death which till then I had always considered as at a distance, now presented itself to me such as it appears to sinners. I began to dread the wrath of God, now I was going to experience it; and I repented I had made no better use of his grace. Those tender letters I have wrote to you, and those passionate conversations I have had with you, gave me as much pain now as they formerly did pleasure. Ah! miserable *Heloise*, said I, if it is a crime to give one's self up to such soft transports, and if after this life is ended punishment certainly follows them, why didst thou not resist so dangerous an inclination? Think on the tortures that are prepared for thee; consider with terror that store of torments, and recollect at the same time those pleasures which thy deluded soul thought so entrancing. Ah! pursued I, dost thou not almost despair for having rioted in such false pleasure? In short, *Abelard*, imagine all the remorse of mind I suffered, and you will not be astonished at my change.

Solitude is insupportable to a mind which is not easy, its troubles increase in the midst of silence, and retirement heightens them. Since I have been shut up within these walls, I have done nothing but wept for our misfortunes. This cloister has resounded with my cries, and like a wretch condemned to eternal slavery, I have worn out my days in grief and sighing. Instead of fulfilling God's merciful design upon me, I have offended him; I have looked upon this sacred refuge like a frightful prison, and have borne with unwillingness the yoke of the Lord. Instead of sanctifying myself by a life of penitence, I have confirmed my reprobation. What a fatal wandering! But *Abelard*, I have torn off the bandage which blinded me, and if I dare rely upon the emotions which I have felt, I have made myself worthy of your esteem. You are no more that amorous *Abelard*, who, to gain a private conversation with me by night, used incessantly to contrive new ways to deceive the vigilance of our observers. The misfortune, which happened to you after so many happy moments, gave you a horror for vice, and you instantly consecrated the rest of your days to virtue and seemed to submit to this necessity willingly. I indeed, more tender than you, and more sensible of soft pleasures, bore this misfortune with extreme impatience. You have heard my exclamations against your enemies; you have seen my whole resentment in those Letters I wrote to you; it was this, without doubt, which deprived me of the esteem of my *Abelard*. You were alarmed at my transport, and if you will confess the truth, you, perhaps, despaired of my salvation. You could not foresee that *Heloise* would conquer so reigning a passion; but you have been deceived, *Abelard*; my weakness, when supported by grace, hath not hindered me from obtaining a complete victory. Restore me, then, to your good opinion; your own piety ought to solicit you to this.

But what secret trouble rises in my soul, what unthought-of motion opposes the resolution I formed of sighing no more for *Abelard*? Just Heaven! have I not yet triumphed over my love? Unhappy *Heloise*! as long as thou drawest a breath it is decreed thou must love *Abelard*: weep unfortunate wretch that thou art, thou never had a more just occasion. Now I ought to die with grief. Grace had overtaken me, and I had promised to be faithful to it, but I now perjure myself, and sacrifice even grace to *Abelard*. This sacrilegious Sacrifice fills up the measure of my iniquities. After this can I hope God should open to me the treasures of his mercy? Have I not tired out his forgiveness? I began to offend him from the moment I first saw *Abelard*; an unhappy sympathy engaged us both in a criminal commerce; and God raised us up an enemy to separate us. I lament and hate the misfortune which hath lighted upon us and adore the cause. Ah! I ought rather to explain this accident as the secret ordinance of Heaven, which disapproved of our engagement, and apply myself to extirpate my passion. How much better were it entirely to forget the object of it, than to preserve the memory of it, so fatal to the quiet of my life and salvation? Great God! shall *Abelard* always possess my thoughts? can I never free myself from those chains which bind me to him? But, perhaps, I am unreasonably afraid; virtue directs all my motions, and they are all subject to grace, Fear no more, dear *Abelard*; I have no longer any of those sentiments which, being described in my Letters, have occasioned you so much trouble. I will no more endeavour, by the relation of those pleasures our new-born passion gave us, to awaken that criminal fondness you may have for me; I free you from all your oaths; forget the names of Lover and husband but keep always that of Father. I expect no more from you those tender protestations, and those letters so proper to keep up the commerce of love. I demand nothing of you but spiritual advice and wholesome directions. The path of holiness, however thorny it may be, will yet appear agreeable when I walk in your steps. You will always find me ready to follow you. I shall read with more pleasure the letters in which you shall describe to me the advantages of virtue than ever I did those by which you so artfully instilled the fatal poison of our passion. You cannot now be silent without a crime. When I was possessed with so violent a love, and pressed you so earnestly to write to me, how many letters did I send you before I could obtain one from you? You denied me in my misery the only comfort which was left me, because you thought it pernicious. You endeavoured by severities to force me to forget you; nor can I blame you; but now you have nothing to fear. A lucky disease which providence seemed to have chastised me with for my sanctification, hath done what all human efforts, and your cruelty in vain attempted. I see now the vanity of that happiness which we had set our hearts upon, as if we were never to have lost it. What fears, what uneasiness, have we been obliged to suffer!

No, Lord, there is no pleasure upon earth but that which virtue gives! The heart, amidst all worldly delights, feels a sting; it is uneasy and restless till fixed on thee. What have I not suffered, *Abelard*, while I kept alive in my retirement those fires which ruined me in the world? I saw with horror the walls which surrounded me; the hours seemed as long as years. I repented a thousand times the having buried myself here; but since grace has opened my eyes all the scene is changed. Solitude looks charming, and the tranquillity which I behold here enters my very heart. In the satisfaction of doing my duty I feel a pleasure above all that riches, pomp, or sensuality, could afford. My quiet has indeed cost me dear; I have bought it even at the price of my love; I have offered a violent sacrifice, and which seemed above my power. I have torn you from my heart; and, be not jealous, God reigns there in your stead, who ought always to have possessed it entire. Be content with having a place in my mind, which you shall never lose; I shall always take a secret pleasure in thinking of you and esteem it a glory to obey those rules you shall give me.

This very moment I receive a letter from you: I will read it, and answer it immediately. You shall see, by my exactness in writing to you, that you are always dear to me.—You very obligingly reproach me for delaying so long to write you any news; my illness must excuse that. I omit no opportunities of giving you marks of my remembrance. I thank you for the uneasiness you say my silence caused you, and the kind fears you express concerning my health. Yours, you tell me is but weakly, and you thought lately you should have died. With what indifference, cruel man! do you acquaint me with a thing so certain to afflict me? I told you in my former letter how unhappy I should be if you died; and if you loved me, you would moderate the rigour of your austere life. I represented to you the occasion I had for your advice, and consequently, the reason there was you should take care of yourself. But I will not tire you with the repetition of the same thing. *You desire us not to forget you in your prayers.* Ah! dear *Abelard*, you may depend upon the zeal of this society; it is devoted to you, and you cannot justly charge it with forgetfulness. You are our father, we your children; you are our guide, and we resign ourselves with assurance in your piety. We impose no pennance on ourselves but what you recommend, lest we should rather follow an indiscreet zeal than solid virtue. In a word, nothing is thought rightly done if without *Abelard's* approbation. You inform me of one thing that perplexes me, that you have heard that some of our sisters gave bad examples, and that there is a general looseness amongst them. Ought this to seem strange to you, who know how monasteries are filled now-a-days? Do fathers consult the inclinations of their children when they settle them? Are not interest and policy their only rules? This is the reason that monasteries are often filled with those who are a scandal to them. But I conjure you to tell me what are the irregularities you have heard of, and to teach me a proper remedy for them. I have not yet observed that looseness you mention; when I have, I will take due care. I walk my rounds every night, and make those I catch abroad return to their chambers; for I remember all the adventures which happened in the monasteries near Paris. You end your letter with a general deploring of your unhappiness, and wish for death as the end of a troublesome life. Is it possible a genius so great as yours should never get above his past misfortunes? What would the world say should they read your letters as I do? would they consider the noble motive of your retirement, or not rather think you had shut yourself up only to lament the condition to which my uncle's revenge had reduced you? What would your young pupils say who came so far to hear you, and prefer your severe lectures to the softness of a worldly life, if they should see you secretly a slave to your passions, and sensible of all those weakness from which your rules can secure them? This *Abelard* they so much admire, this great personage which guides them, would lose his fame, and become the scorn of his pupils. If these reasons are not sufficient to give you constancy in your misfortunes, cast your eyes upon me, and admire my resolution of shutting myself up by your example. I was young when we were separated, and (if I dare believe what you were always telling me) worthy of any gentleman's affections. If I had loved nothing in *Abelard* but sensual pleasure, a thousand agreeable young men might have comforted me upon my loss of him. You know what I have done, excuse me therefore from repeating it. Think of those assurances I gave you of loving you with the utmost tenderness. I dried your tears with kisses; and because you were less powerful I became less reserved. Ah! if you had loved with delicacy the oaths I made, the transports I accompanied them with, the innocent caresses I profusely gave you, all this, sure, might have comforted you. Had you observed me to grow by degrees indifferent to you, you might have had reason to despair; but you never received greater marks of my passion than after that cruel revenge upon you.

Let me see no more in your letters, dear *Abelard*, such murmurs against Fortune; you are not the only one she has persecuted, and you ought to forget her outrages. What a shame is it for a philosopher not to be comforted for an accident which might happen to any man! Govern yourself by my example. I was born with violent passions; I daily strive with the most tender emotions, and glory in triumphing and subjecting them to reason. Must a weak mind fortify one that is so much superior? But whither am I transported? Is this discourse directed to my dear *Abelard?* one that practices all those virtues he teaches? If you complain of Fortune, it is not so much that you feel her strokes, as that you cannot show your enemies how much to blame they were in attempting to hurt you. Leave them, *Abelard*, to exhaust their malice, and continue to charm your auditors. Discover those treasures of learning Heaven seems to have reserved for you: your enemies, struck with the splendor of your reasoning, will do you justice. How happy should I be could I see all the world as entirely persuaded of your probity as I am! Your learning is allowed by all the world; your greatest enemies confess you are ignorant of nothing that the mind of man is capable of knowing.

My dear husband! (this is the last time I shall use that expression) shall I never see you again? shall I never have the pleasure of embracing you before death? What doth thou say, wretched *Heloise?* dost thou know what thou desirest? Canst thou behold those lovely eyes without recollecting those amorous glances which have been so fatal to thee? canst thou view that majestic air of *Abelard* without entertaining a jealousy of every one that sees so charming a man? that mouth, which cannot be looked upon without desire? In short all the person of *Abelard* cannot be viewed by any woman without danger. Desire therefore no more to see *Abelard*. If the memory of him has caused thee so much trouble, *Heloise*, what will not his presence do? what desires will it not excite in thy soul? how will it be possible for thee to keep thy reason at the sight of so amiable a man? I will own to you what makes the greatest pleasure I have in my retirement: After having passed the day in thinking of you, full of the dear idea, I give myself up at night to sleep. Then it is that *Heloise*, who dares not without trembling think of you by day, resigns herself entirely to the pleasure of hearing you and speaking to you. I see you, *Abelard*, and glut my eyes with the sight. Sometimes you entertain me with the story of your secret troubles and grievances, and create in me a sensible sorrow; sometimes forgetting the perpetual obstacles to our desires, you press me to make you happy, and I easily yield to your transports. Sleep gives you what your enemies rage has deprived you of; and our souls, animated with the same passion, are sensible of the same pleasure. But, oh! you delightful illusion, soft errors, how soon do you vanish away! At my awaking I open my eyes and see no *Abelard*; I stretch out my arm to take hold of him, but he is not there; I call him, he hears me not. What a fool am I to tell you my dreams, who are sensible of these pleasures? But do you, *Abelard*, never see *Heloise* in your sleep? how does she appear to you? do you entertain her with the same language as formerly when Fulbert committed her to your care? when you awake are you pleased or sorry? Pardon me; *Abelard*, pardon a mistaken lover. I must no more expect that vivacity from you which once animated all your actions. 'Tis no more time to require from you a perfect correspondence of desires. We have bound ourselves to severe austerities, and must follow them, let them cost us ever so dear. Let us think of our duties in these rigours, and make a good use of that necessity which keeps us separate. You *Abelard*, will happily finish your course; your desires and ambition will be no obstacles to your salvation. *Heloise* only must lament, she only must weep, without being certain whether all her tears will be available or not to her salvation.

I had like to have ended my letter without acquainting you with what happened here a few days ago. A young nun, who was one of those who are forced to take up with a convent without any examination. whether it will suit with their tempers or not, is by a stratagem I knew nothing of, escaped, and, as they say, fled with a young gentleman she was in love with into England. I have ordered all the house to conceal the matter. Ah, *Abelard*! if you were near us these disorders would not happen. All the sisters, charmed with seeing and hearing you, would think of nothing but practicing your rules and directions. The young nun had never formed so criminal a design as that of breaking her vows, had you been at our head to exhort us to live holily. If your eyes were witnesses of our actions, they would be innocent.

When we slipt, you would lift us up, and establish us by your counsels; we should march with sure steps in the rough paths of virtue. I begin to perceive; *Abelard*, that I take too much pleasure in writing to you. I ought to burn my letter. It shows you I am still engaged in a deep passion for you, though at the beginning of it I designed to persuade you of the contrary. I am sensible of the motions both of grace and passion, and by turns yield to each. Have pity, *Abelard*, of the condition to which you have brought me, and make, in some measure, the latter days of my life as quiet as the first have been uneasy and disturbed.

LETTER VI.

ABELARD TO HELOISE.

Abelard, having at last conquered the remains of his unhappy passion, had determined to put an end to so dangerous a correspondence as that between *Heloise* and himself. The following Letter therefore, though written with no less concern than his former, is free from mixtures of a worldly passion, and is full of the warmest sentiments of piety, and the most moving exhortations.

Write no more to me, *Heloise*; write no more to me; it is a time to end a commerce which makes our mortifications of no advantage to us. We retired from the world to sanctify ourselves; and by a conduit directly contrary to Christian morality, we become odious to Jesus Christ. Let us no more deceive ourselves; by flattering ourselves with the remembrance of our past pleasures, we shall make our lives troublesome, and we shall be incapable of relishing the sweets of solitude. Let us make a good use of our austerities, and no longer preserve the ideas of our crimes amongst the severities of penitence. Let a mortification of body and mind, a strick fasting, continual solitude, profound and holy meditations, and a sincere love of God, succeed our former irregularities.

Let us try to carry religious perfection to a very difficult point. 'Tis beautiful to find, in Christianity minds so disengaged from the earth, from the creatures and themselves, that they seem to act independently of those bodies they are joined to, and to use them as their slaves. We can never raise ourselves to too great heights when God is the object. Be our endeavours ever so great, they will always come short of reaching that exalted dignity, which even our apprehensions cannot reach. Let us act for God's glory, independent of the creatures or ourselves, without any regard to our own desires, or the sentiments of others. Were we in this temper of mind, *Heloise*, I would willingly make my abode at the Paraclete. My earnest care for a house I have founded would draw a thousand blessings on it. I would instruct it by my words, and animate it by my example. I would watch over the lives of my sisters, and would command nothing but what I myself would perform. I would direct you to pray, meditate, labour and keep vows of silence; and I would myself pray, meditate, labour and be silent.

However, when I spoke, it should be to lift you up when you should fall, to strengthen you in your weaknesses, to enlighten you in that darkness and obscurity which might at any time surprise you. I would comfort you under those severities used by persons of great virtue. I would moderate the vivacity of your zeal and piety, and give your virtue an even temperament. I would point out those duties which you ought to know, and satisfy you in those doubts which the weakness of your reason might occasion. I would be your master and father; and, by a marvellous talent, I would become lively, flow, soft or severe, according to the different characters of those I should guide in the painful path of Christian perfection.

But whither does my vain imagination carry me?

Ah? *Heloise*! how far are we from such a happy temper? Your heart still burns with that fatal fire which you cannot extinguish, and mine is full of trouble and uneasiness. Think not, *Heloise*, that I enjoy here a perfect peace: I will, for the last time open my heart to you. I am not yet disengaged from you; I fight against my excessive tenderness for you; yet in spite of all endeavours, the remaining frailty makes me but too sensible of your sorrows, and gives me a share in them. Your Letters have indeed moved me; I could not read with indifference characters wrote by that dear hand. I sigh, I weep, and all my reason is, scarce sufficient to conceal my weakness from my pupils. This, unhappy *Heloise*! is the miserable condition of *Abelard*. The world, which generally errs in its notion, thinks I am easy, and as if I had loved only in you the gratification of sense, imagines I have now forgot you; but what a mistake is this! People, indeed, did not mistake in thinking, when we separated, that shame and grief for having been so cruelly used made me abandon the world. It was not, as you know, a sincere repentance for having offended God which inspired me with a design of retiring; however, I considered the accident which happened to us as a secret design of Providence to punish our crimes; and only looked upon Fulbert as the instrument of Divine vengeance. Grace drew me into an asylum, where I might yet have remained, if the rage of my enemies would have permitted. I have endured all their persecutions, not doubting but God himself raised them up in order to purify me.

When he saw me perfectly obedient to his holy will, he permitted that I should justify my doctrine. I made its purity public, and showed in the end that my faith was not only orthodox, but also perfectly clear from even the suspicion of novelty.

I should be happy if I had none to fear but my enemies, and no other hinderance to my salvation but their calumny: but, *Heloise*, you make me tremble. Your Letters declare to me that you are enslaved to a fatal passion; and yet if you cannot conquer it you cannot be saved; and what part would you have me take in this case? Would you have me stifle the inspirations of the Holy Ghost? shall I, to soothe you dry up those tears which the evil spirit makes you shed? Shall this be the fruit of my meditations? No; let us be more firm in our resolutions. We have not retired but in order to lament our sins, and to gain heaven; let us then resign ourselves to God with all our heart.

I know every thing in the beginning is difficult, but it is glorious to undertake the beginning of a great action, and that glory increases proportionably as the difficulties are more considerable. We ought upon this account to surmount bravely all obstacles which might hinder us in the practice of Christian virtue. In a monastery men are proved as gold in the furnace. No one can continue long there unless he bear worthily the yoke of our Lord.

Attempt to break those shameful chains which bind you to the flesh; and, if by the assistance of grace you are so happy as to accomplish this, I intreat you to think of me in your prayers. Endeavour with all your strength to be the pattern of a perfect Christian. It is difficult, I confess, but not impossible; and I expect this beautiful triumph from your teachable disposition. If your first endeavours prove weak, give not yourself up to despair; that would be cowardice: besides, I would have you informed, that you must necessarily take great pains; because you drive to conquer a terrible enemy, to extinguish raging fire, and to reduce to subjection your dearest affections. You must fight against your own desires; be not therefore pressed down with the weight of your corrupt nature: you have to do with a cunning adversary, who will use all means to seduce you; be always upon your guard; While we live we are exposed to temptations: this made a great saint say, that *the whole life of man was a temptation*. The devil, who never sleeps, walks continually around us, in order to surprise us on some unguarded side, and enters into our soul to destroy it.

However perfect any one may be, yet he may fall into temptations, and, perhaps, into such as may be useful. Nor is it wonderful that men should never be exempt from them, because he hath always within himself their force, concupiscence. Scarce are we delivered from one temptation, but another attacks us. Such is the lot of the posterity of Adam, that they should always have something to suffer, because they have forfeited their primitive happiness. We vainly flatter ourselves that we shall conquer temptations by flying; if we join not patience and humility, we shall torment ourselves to no purpose. We shall more certainly compass our end by imploring God's assistance than by using any means drawn from ourselves.

Be constant, *Heloise*; trust in God, and you will fall into few temptations: whenever they shall come, stifle them in their birth; let them not take root in your heart. Apply remedies to a disease, said an Ancient, in its beginning; for when it hath gained strength medicines will be unavailable. Temptations have their degrees; they are at first mere thoughts, and do not appear dangerous; the imagination receives them without any fears; a pleasure is formed out of them; we pause upon it, and at last we yield to it.

Do you now, *Heloise*, applaud my design of making you walk in the steps of the saints? do my words give you any relish for penitence? have you not remorse for your wanderings? and do you not wish you could like Magdalen, wash our Saviour's feet with your tears? If you have not these ardent emotions, pray that he would inspire them. I shall never cease to recommend you in my prayers, and always beseech him to assist you in your design of dying holily. You have quitted the world, and what object was worthy to detain you there? Lift up your eyes always to him so whom you have consecrated the rest of your days. Life upon this earth is misery. The very necessities to which our body is subject here are matter of affliction to a saint. *Lord,* said the Royal Prophet, *deliver me from my necessities*! They are wretched who do not know themselves for such, and yet they are more wretched who know their misery, and do not hate the corruption of the age. What fools are men to engage themselves to earthly things! they will be undeceived one day, and will know but too late how much they have been too blame in loving such false good. Persons truly pious do not thus mistake, they are disengaged from all sensual pleasures, and raise their desires to heaven. Begin *Heloise*; put your design in execution without delay; you have yet time enough to work out your salvation. Love Christ, and despise yourself for his sake. He would possess your heart, and be the sole object of your sighs and tears; seek for no comfort but in him. If you do not free yourself from me, you will fall with me; but if you quit me, and give up yourself to him, you will be stedfast and immoveable. If you force the Lord to forsake you, you will fall into distress; but if you be ever faithful to him, you will always be in joy. Magdalen wept, as thinking the Lord had forsaken her; but Martha said, See, the Lord calls you. Be diligent in your duty, and obey faithfully the motions of his grace, and Jesus will remain always with you.

Attend, *Heloise*, to some instructions I have to give you. You are at the head of a society, and you know there is this difference between those who lead a private life and such as are charged with the conduct of others; that the first need only labour for their own sanctification, and, in acquitting themselves of their duties, are not obliged to practise all the virtues in such an apparent manner; whereas they who have the conduct of others intruded to them, ought by their example to engage them to do all the good they are capable of in their condition. I beseech you to attend to this truth, and so to follow it, as that your whole life may be a perfect model of that of a religious recluse.

God, who heartily desires our salvation, hath made all the means of it easy to us; In the *Old Testament* he hath written in the Tables of the Law what he requires of us, that we might not be bewildered in seeking after his will. In the *New Testament* he hath written that law of grace in our hearts, to the intent that it might be always present with us; and, knowing the weakness and incapacity of our nature, he hath given us grace to perform his will; and, as if this were not enough, he hath, at all times, in all dates of the church, raised up men who, by their exemplary life, might excite others to their duty. To effect this, he hath chosen persons of every age, sex, and condition. Strive now to unite in yourself all those virtues which have been scattered in these different states. Have the purity of virgins, the austerity of anchorites, the zeal of pastors and bishops, and the constancy of martyrs. Be exact in the course of your whole life to fulfil the duties of a holy and enlightened superior, and then death, which is commonly considered as terrible, will appear agreeable to you.

The death of his saints, says the Prophet, *is precious in the sight of the Lord.* Nor is it difficult to comprehend why their death should have this advantage over that of sinners. I have remarked three things which might have given the Prophet an occasion of speaking thus. First, Their resignation to the will of God. Secondly, The continuation of their good works. And, lastly, The triumph they gain over the devil.

A saint, who has accustomed himself to submit to the will of God, yields to death without reluctance. He waits with joy (says St. Gregory) for the Judge who is to reward him; he fears not to quit this miserable mortal life, in order to begin an immortal happy one. It is not so with the sinner, says the same Father; he fears, and with reason, he trembles, at the approach of the least sickness; death is terrible to him, because he cannot bear the presence of an offended Judge; and having so often abused the grace of God, he sees no way to avoid the punishment due to his sins.

The saints have besides this advantage over sinners that having made works of piety familiar to them during their life, they exercise them without trouble, and having gained new strength against the devil every time they overcome him, they will find themselves in a condition at the hour of death to obtain that victory over him, on which depends all eternity, and the blessed union of their souls with their Creator.

I hope, *Heloise*, that after having deplored the irregularities of your past life, you will die (as the Prophet prayed) the death of the righteous. Ah! how few are there who make their end after this manner! and why? It is because there are so few who love the Cross of Christ. Every one would be saved, but few will use those means which Religion prescribes. And yet we can be saved by nothing but the Cross, why then do we refuse to bear it? Hath not our Saviour borne it before us, and died for us, to the end that we might also bear it and desire to die also? All the saints have been afflicted; and our Saviour himself did not pass one hour of his life without some sorrow. Hope not, therefore to be exempted from sufferings. The Cross, *Heloise*, is always at hand, but take care that you do not bear it with regret; for by so doing you will make it more heavy, and you will be oppressed by it unprofitably. On the contrary, if you bear it with affection and courage, all your sufferings will create in you a holy confidence, whereby you will find comfort in God. Hear our Saviour who says: "My child renounce yourself, take up your cross and follow me." Oh, *Heloise*! do you doubt? Is not your soul ravished at so saving a command? are you deaf to his voice? are you insensible to words so full of kindness? Beware, *Heloise*, of refusing a husband who demands you, and is more to be feared, if you slight his affection, than any profane lover. Provoked at your contempt and ingratitude, he will turn his love into anger, and make you feel his vengeance, How will you sustain his presence when you shall stand before his tribunal? He will reproach you for having despised his grace; he will represent to you his sufferings for you. What answer can you make? he will then be implacable. He will say to you, Go, proud creature, dwell in everlasting flames. I separated you from the world to purify you in solitude, and you did not second my design; I endeavoured to save you, and you took pains to destroy yourself; go wretch, and take the portion of the reprobates.

Oh, *Heloise*, prevent these terrible words, and avoid by a holy course, the punishment prepared for sinners. I dare not give you a description of those dreadful torments which ere the consequences of a life of guilt. I am filled with horror when they offer themselves to my imagination: and yet *Heloise* I can conceive nothing which can reach the tortures of the damned. The fire which we see upon earth is but the shadow of that which burns them; and without enumerating their endless pains, the loss of God which they feel increases all their torments. Can any one sin who is persuaded of this? My God! can we dare to offend thee? Tho' the riches of thy mercy could not engage us to love thee, the dread of being thrown into such an abyss of misery would restrain us from doing any thing which might displease thee?

I question not, *Heloise*, but you will hereafter apply yourself in good earnest to the business of your salvation: this ought to be your whole concern. Banish me, therefore, for ever from your heart; it is the best advice I can give you: for the remembrance of a person we have loved criminally cannot but be hurtful, whatever advances we have made in the ways of virtue. When you have extirpated your unhappy inclination towards me, the practice of every virtue will become easy; and when at last your life is conformable to that of Christ, death will be desireable to you. Your soul will joyfully leave this body, and direct its flight to heaven. Then you will appear with confidence before your Saviour. You will not read characters of your reprobation written in the book of life; but you will hear your Saviour say, Come, partake of my glory, and enjoy the eternal reward I have appointed for those virtues you have practised.

Farewell *Heloise*. This is the last advice of your dear *Abelard*; this is the last time, let me persuade you to follow the holy rules of the Gospel. Heaven grant that your heart, once so sensible of my love, may now yield to be directed by my zeal! May the idea of your loving *Abelard*, always present to your mind, be now changed into the image of *Abelard* truly penitent! and may you shed as many tears for your salvation as you have done during the course of our misfortunes!

ELOISA to ABELARD

BY MR POPE.

In these deep solitudes and awful cells.
Where heav'nly-pensive Contemplation dwells,
And ever-musing Melancholy reigns;
What means this tumult in a Vestal's veins?
Why rove my thoughts beyond this last retreat?
Why feels my heart its long-forgotten beat?
Yet, yet I love!——From Abelard *it came,*
And Eloisa *yet must kiss the name.*
 Dear fatal name! rest ever onreveal'd,
Nor pass those lips in holy silence seas'd:
Hide it, my heart, within that close disguise,
Where mix'd with God's, his lov'd idea lyes;
Oh write it not, my hand—the name appears
Already written—wash it out, my tears!
In vain lost Eloisa *weeps and prays,*
Her heart still dictates, and her hand obeys.
 Relentless walls! whose darksome round contains
Repentant sighs, and voluntary pains:
Ye rugged rocks! which holy knees have worn;
Ye grotes and caverns shagg'd with horrid thorn!
Shrines! where their vigils pale-ey'd virgins keep,

And pitying saints, whose statues learn to weep!
Tho' cold like you unmov'd and silent grown,
I have not yet forgot myself to stone.
Heav'n claims me all in vain, while he has part,
Still rebel Nature holds out half my heart;
Nor pray'rs nor fasts its stubborn pulse restrain,
Nor tears, for ages taught to flow in vain.
 Soon as thy Letters, trembling, I unclose,
That well-known name awakens all my woes.
Oh name for ever sad! for ever dear!
Still breath'd in sighs, still utter'd with a tear.
I tremble too where'er my own I find,
Some dire misfortune follows close behind.
Line after line my gushing eyes o'erflow,
Led through a sad variety of woe:
Now warm in love, now with'ring in thy bloom,
Lost in a convent's solitary gloom!
There stern religion quench'd th' unwilling flame.
There died the best of passions, love and same.
 Yet write, oh write me all, that I may join
Griefs to thy griefs, and echo sighs to thine.
Nor foes nor fortune take this pow'r away;
And is my Abelard less kind than they?
Tears still are mine, and those I need not spare,
Love but demands what else were shed in pray'r;
No happier talk these faded eyes pursue;
To read and weep is all they now can do.
 Then share thy pain, allow that sad relief;
Ah, more than share it! give me all thy grief.
Heav'n first taught letters for some wretch's aid,
Some banish'd lover, or some captive maid;
They live they speak, they breathe what love inspires,
Warm from the soul, and faithful to its fires,
The virgin's wish without her fears impart,
Excuse the blush, and pour out all the heart,
Speed the soft intercourse from soul to soul,
And waft a sigh from Indus to the Pole.

Thou know'st how guiltless first I met thy flame,
When Love approach'd me under Friendship's name;
My fancy form'd thee of angelic kind,
Some emanations of th' all-beauteous Mind.
Those smiling eyes, attemp'ring every ray,
Shone sweetly lambent with celestial day.
Guiltless I gaz'd; Heav'n listen'd while you sung;
And truths divine came mended from that tongue,
From lip like those what precepts fail'd to move?
Too soon they taught me 'twas no sin to love:
Back through the paths of pleasing sense I ran,
Nor wish'd an angel whom I lov'd a man.
Dim and remote the joys of saints I see,
Nor envy them that heav'n I lose for thee.
How oft', when prest to marriage, have I said,
Curse on all laws but those which Love has made!
Love, free as air, at sight of human ties,
Spreads his light wings, and in a moment flies.
Let wealth, let honour, wait the wedded dame,
August her deed, and sacred be her fame;
Before true passion all those views remove,
Fame, wealth, and honour! what are you to love?
The jealous God, when we profane his fires,
Those restless passions in revenge inspires,
And bids them make mistaken mortals groan,
Who seek in love for ought but love alone.
Should at my feet the world's great master fall,
Himself, his throne, his world, I'd scorn 'em all;
Not Ceasar's empress would I deign to prove;
No, make me mistress to the man I love;
If there be yet another name more free,
More fond, than Mistress, make me that to thee!
Oh happy state! when souls each other draw.
When love is liberty, and nature law,
All then is full possessing and possess'd,
No craving void left akeing in the breast?
Ev'n thought meets thought, ere from the lips it part,

And each warm wish springs mutual from the heart.
This sure is bliss, (if bliss on earth there be,)
And once the lot of Abelard *and me.*
Alas, how chang'd! what sudden horrors rise!
A naked lover bound and bleeding lyes!
Where, where was Eloisa? *her voice, her hand,*
Her poinard, had oppos'd the dire command.
Barbarian, stay! that bloody stroke restrain;
The crime was common, common be the pain.
I can no more; by shame, by rage, suppress'd,
Let tears and burning blushes speak the rest.
Canst thou forget that sad, that solemn day,
When victims at yon altar's foot we lay?
Canst thou forget what tears that moment fell,
When, warm in youth, I bade the world farewell?
As, with cold lips I kiss'd the sacred veil,
The shrines all trembled, and the lamps grew pale:
Heav'n scarces believ'd the conquest it survey'd,
And saints with wonder heard the vows I made.
Yet then, to those dread altars as I drew,
Not on the Cross my eyes were fix'd, but you:
Not grace, or zeal, love only was my call,
And if I lose thy love, I lose my all.
Come! with thy looks, thy words, relieve my woe;
Those still at least are left thee to bestow.
Still on that breast enamour'd let me lye,
Still drink delicious poison from thy eye,
Pant on thy lip, and to thy heart be press'd;
Give all thou canst——and let me dream the rest,
Ah, no! instruct me other joys to prize,
With other beauties charm my partial eyes.
Full in my view set all the bright abode,
And make my soul quit Abelard *for God.*
Ah! think at least thy flock deserves thy care,
Plants of thy hand, and children of thy pray'r.
From the false world in early youth they fled,
By thee to mountains, wilds, and deserts led.

You rais'd these hallow'd walls; the desart smil'd,
And Paradise was open'd in the wild.
No weeping orphan saw his father's stores
Our shines irradiate, or emblaze the floors:
No silver saints, by dying misers given,
Here brib'd the rage of ill-requited Heav'n:
But such plain roofs as piety could raise,
And only vocal with the maker's praise.
In these lone walls (their days eternal bound)
These moss-grown domes with spiry turrets crown'd,
Where awful arches make a noon-day night,
And the dim windows shed a solemn light;
Thy eyes diffus'd a reconciling ray,
And gleams of glory brighten'd all the day,
But now no face divine contentment wears,
'Tis all blank sadness, or continual tears.
See how the force of others' pray'rs I try,
(Oh pious fraud of am'rous charity!)
But why should I on others' prayers depend?
Come thou, my Father, Brother, Husband, Friend!
Ah, let thy Handmaid, Sister, Daughter, move,
And all those tender Names in one, thy Love!
The darksome pines, that o'er yon rocks reclin'd
Wave high, and murmur to the hollow wind,
The wand'ring streams that shine between the hills,
The grotes that echo to the tinkling rills,
The dying gales that pant upon the trees,
The lakes that quiver to the curling breeze;
No more these scenes my meditation aid,
Or lull to rest the visionary maid.
But o'er the twilight groves, and dusky caves,
Long founding aisles, and intermingled graves,
Black Melancholy sits, and round her throws
A death like silence, and a dread repose:
Her gloomy presence saddens all the scene.
Shades ev'ry flow'r, and darkens ev'ry green,
Deepens the murmur of the falling floods,
And breathes a browner horror on the woods,

Yet here for ever, ever must I stay;
Sad proof how well a lover can obey!
Death, only death, can break the lasting chain;
And here, ev'n then, shall my cold dust remain;
Here all its frailties, all its flames resign,
And wait, till 'tis no sin to mix with thine.
Ah, wretch! believ'd the spouse of God in vain,
Confess'd within the slave of love and man.
Assist me, Heav'n! But whence, arose that pray'r?
Sprung it from piety, or from despair?
Ev'n here, where frozen Chastity retires,
Love finds an altar for forbidden fires.
I ought to grieve, but cannot what I ought;
I mourn the lover, not lament the fault;
I view my crime, but kindle at the view,
Repent old pleasures, and solicit new;
Now turn'd to Heav'n, I weep my past offence,
Now think of thee, and curse my innocence.
Of all Affliction taught a lover yet,
'Tis sure the hardest science to forget!
How shall I lose the sin, yet, keep the sense.
And love th' offender, yet detest th' offence?
How the dear object from the crime remove,
Or how distinguish penitence from love?
Unequal talk! a passion to resign,
For hearts so touched, so pierc'd, so lost as mine.
Ere such a soul regains its peaceful slate.
How often must it love, how often hate!
How often hope, despair, resent, regret.
Conceal, disdain—do all things but forget!
But let Heav'n seize it, all at once 'tis fir'd,
Not touched but rapt; not waken'd but inspir'd!
Oh come! oh teach me nature to subdue.
Renounce my love, my life, myself—and you.
Fill my fond heart with God alone, for he
Alone can rival, can succeed to thee.
How happy is the blameless Vestal's lot?
The world forgetting, by the world forgot:

Eternal sunshine of the spotless mind!
Each pray'r accepted, and each wish resign'd;
Labour and rest, that equal periods keep,
'Obedient slumbers that can wake and weep;
Desires compos'd, affections ever even;
Tears that delight, and sighs that waft to heav'n.
Grace shines around her with serenest beams,
And whisp'ring angels prompt her golden dreams,
For her the house prepares the bridal ring,
For her white virgins hymeneals sing,
For her th' unfading rose of Eden blooms,
And wings of seraphs shed divine perfumes;
To sounds of heavenly harps she dies away,
And melts in visions of eternal day.
Far other dreams my erring soul employ,
Far other raptures of unholy joy:
When at the close of each sad sorrowing day
Fancy restores what Vengeance snatch'd away,
Then Conscience sleeps, and leaving Nature free,
All my loose soul unbounded springs to thee.
O curs'd dear horrors of all-conscious Night!
How glowing guilt exalts the keen delight!
Provoking daemons all restraint remove,
And stir within me ev'ry source of love,
I hear thee, view thee, gaze o'er all thy charms,
And round thy phantoms glue my clasping arms.
I wake——no more I hear, no more I view,
The phantom flies me as unkind as you.
I call aloud; it hears not what I say;
I stretch my empty arms; it glides away.
To dream once more I close my willing eyes;
Ye soft illusions, dear deceits, arise!
Alas no more!——Methinks we wand'ring go,
Thro' dreary waftes, and weep each other's woe
Where round some moulding tow'r pale ivy creeps,
And low-brow'd rocks hang nodding o'er the deeps.
Sudden you mount, you beckon from the skies:
Clouds interpose, waves roar, and winds arise.

I shriek, start up, the same sad prospect find
And wake to all the griefs I left behind.
For thee the fates, severely kind, ordain
A cool suspence from pleasure and from pain;
Thy life a long dead calm of fix'd repose;
No pulse that riots, and no blood that glows;
Still as the sea, ere winds were taught to blow,
Or moving Spirit bade the waters flow;
Soft as the slumbers of a saint forgiv'n,
And mild as opening gleams of promis'd heav'n.
 Come, Abelard! *for what hast thou to dread?*
The torch of Venus burns not for the dead.
Nature stands check'd; Religion disapproves;
Ev'n thou art cold——yet Eloisa *loves.*
Ah hopeless, lasting flames! like those that burn.
To light the dead, and warm th' unfruitful urn.
What scenes appear! where e'er I turn my view.
The dear ideas where I fly pursue,
Rise in the grove, before the altar rise,
Stain all my soul, and wanton in my eyes.
I waste the matin lamp in sighs for thee,
Thy image steals between my God and me;
Thy voice I seem in ev'ry hymn to hear,
With ev'ry bead I drop too soft a tear.
When from the censer clouds of fragrance roll,
And swelling organs lift the rising soul,
One thought of thee puts all the pomp to flight,
Priests, tapers, temples; swim before my sight:
In seas of flame my plunging soul is drown'd,
While altars blaze, and angels tremble round.
While prostrate here in humble grief I lye
Kind, virtuous drops, just gathering in my eye,
While praying, trembling, in the dust I roll,
And dawning grace is opening on my soul:
Come, if thou dar'st, all charming as thou art!
Oppose thyself to Heav'n; dispute my heart;
Come, with one glance of those deluding eyes
Blot out each bright idea of the skies;

Take back that grace, those sorrows, and those tears;
Take back my fruitless penitence and prayers;
Snatch me, just mounting, from the blest abode;
Assist the fiend, and tear me from my God!
No, fly me! fly me! far as pole from pole;
Rise Alps between us, and whose oceans roll!
Ah, come not, write not, think not once of me,
Nor share one pang of all I felt for thee,
Thy oaths I quit, thy memory resign;
Forget, renounce me, hate whate'er was mine.
Fair eyes, and tempting looks, which yet I view!
Long-liv'd ador'd ideas, all adieu!
O grace serene! oh virtue heav'nly fair!
Divine oblivion of low-thoughted care!
Fresh blooming Hope, gay daughter of the sky!
And faith, our early immortality!
Enter, each mild, each amicable guest;
Receive and wrap me in eternal rest!
* See in her cell sad Eloisa spread,*
Propt on some tomb, a neighbour of the dead!
In each low wind methinks a spirit calls,
And more than echoes talk along the walls,
Here, as I watch'd the dying lamps around,
From yonder shrine I heard a hollow sound:
'Come, sister, come I (it said, or seem'd to say,)
'Thy place is here, sad sister come away!
'Once like thyself I trembled, wept, and pray'd,
'Love's victim then, though now a sainted maid:
'But all is calm in this eternal sleep;
'Here Grief forgets to groan, and Love to weep;
'Ev'n Superstition loses ev'ry fear:
'For God, not man, absolves our frailties here.'
I come, I come! prepare your roseat bow'rs,
Celestial palm, and ever-blooming flow'rs.
Thither, were sinners may have rest, I go,
Where flames refin'd in breasts seraphic glow:
Thou, Abelard! the last sad office pay,
And smooth my passage to the realms of day;

See my lips tremble, and my eye-balk roll,
Suck my last breath, and catch the flying soul!
Ah no——in sacred vestments may'st thou stand,
The hallow'd taper trembling in thy hand,
Present the Cross before my lifted eye,
Teach me at once, and learn of me to die.
Ah then, the once lov'd Eloisa *see!*
It will be then no crime to gaze on me.
See from my cheek the transient roses fly!
See the last sparkle languish in my eye!
'Till ev'ry motion, pulse, and breath be o'er;
And ev'n my Abelard. *be lov'd no more.*
O death, all eloquent! you only prove
What dust we dote on, when 'tis man we love.
 Then too, when Fate shall thy fair frame destroy?
(That cause of all my guilt, and all my joy)
In trance ecstatic may the pangs be drown'd,
Bright clouds descend, and angels watch thee round,
From opening skies may streaming glories shine,
And saints embrace thee with a love like mine.
May one kind grave unite each hapless name,
And graft my love immortal on thy fame!
Then, ages hence, when all my woes are o'er,
When this rebellious heart shall beat no more.
If ever Chance two wand'ring lovers brings
To Paraclete's *white walls and silver springs,*
O'er the pale marble shall they join their heads.
And drink the falling tears each other sheds;
Then sadly say, with mutual pity mov'd,
"Oh may we never love as these have lov'd!"
From the full choir, when loud Hosannas rise,
And swell the pomp of dreadful sacrifice,
Amid that scene, if some relenting eye
Glance on the stone where our cold relics lye,
Devotion's self shall steal a thought from heav'n,
One human tear shall drop, and be forgiven.
And sure, if Fate some future bard shall join
In sad similitude of griefs like mine,

Condemn'd whole years in absence to deplore,
And image charms he must behold no more;
Such if there be, who loves so long, so well;
Let him our sad, our tender, story tell;
The well-sung woes will smooth my pensive ghost:
He best can paint e'm, who shall feel 'em most.

ABELARD to ELOISA

BY MRS MADAN.

In my dark cell, low prostrate on the ground,
Mourning my crimes, thy Letter entrance found;
Too soon my soul the well-known name confest,
My beating heart sprang fiercely in my breast,
Thro' my whole frame a guilty transport glow'd,
And streaming torrents from my eyes fast flow'd:
 O Eloisa! art thou still the same?
Dost thou still nourish this destructive flame?
Have not the gentle rules of Peace and Heav'n,
From thy soft soul this fatal passion driv'n?
Alas! I thought you disengaged and free;
And can you still, still sigh and weep for me?
What powerful Deity, what hallow'd Shrine,
Can save me from a love, a faith like thine?
Where shall I fly, when not this awful Cave,
Whose rugged feet the surging billows lave;
When not these gloomy cloister's solemn walls,
O'er whose rough sides the languid ivy crawls,
When my dread vews, in vain, their force oppose?
Oppos'd to live—alas!—how vain are vows!
In fruitless penitence I wear away
Each tedious night, and sad revolving day;

I fast, I pray, and, with deceitful art,
Veil thy dear image in my tortur'd heart;
My tortur'd heart conflicting passions move.
I hope despair, repent——yet still I love:
A thousand jarring thoughts my bosom tear;
For, thou, not God, O Eloise! *art there.*
To the false world's deluding pleasures dead,
Nor longer by its wand'ring fires misled,
In learn'd disputes harsh precepts I infuse,
And give the counsel I want pow'r to use.
The rigid maxims of the grave and wife
Have quench'd each milder sparkle of my eyes:
Each lovley feature of this once lov'd face,
By grief revers'd, assumes a sterner grace;
O Eloisa! *should the fates once more,*
Indulgent to my view, thy charms restore,
How from my arms would'st thou with horror start
To miss the form familiar to thy heart;
Nought could thy quick, thy piercing judgment see,
To speak me Abelard——*but love to thee.*
Lean Abstinence, pale Grief, and haggard Care.
The dire attendants of forlorn Despair,
Have Abelard, *the young, the gay, remov'd,*
And in the Hermit funk the man you lov'd,
Wrapt in the gloom these holy mansions shed,
The thorny paths of Penitence I tread;
Lost to the world, from all its int'rests free,
And torn from all my soul held dear in thee,
Ambition with its train of frailties gone,
All loves and forms forget——but thine alone,
Amid the blaze of day, the dusk of night,
My Eloisa *rises to my sight;*
Veil'd as in Paraclete's secluded tow'rs,
The wretched mourner counts the lagging hours;
I hear her sighs, see the swift falling tears,
Weep all her griefs, and pant with all her cares.
O vows! O convent! your stern force impart,
And frown the melting phantom from my heart;

Let other sighs a worthier sorrow show,
Let other tears from sin repentance flow;
Low to the earth my guilty eyes I roll,
And humble to the dust my heaving soul,
Forgiving Pow'r! thy gracious call I meet,
Who first impower'd this rebel heart to beat;
Who thro' this trembling, this offending frame,
For nobler ends inspir'd life's active flame.
O! change the temper of this laboring breast,
And form anew each beating pulse to rest!
Let springing grace, fair faith, and hope remove
The fatal traces of destructive love!
Destructive love from his warm mansions tear,
And leave no traits of Eloisa there!
Are these the wishes of my inmost soul?
Would I its soft, its tend'rest sense controul?
Would I, thus touch'd, this glowing heart refine,
To the cold substance of this marble shrine?
Transform'd like these pale swarms that round me move,
Of blest insensibles—who know no love?
Ah! rather let me keep this hapless flame;
Adieu! false honour, unavailing fame!
Not your harsh rules, but tender love, supplies
The streams that gush from my despairing eyes;
I feel the traitor melt about my heart,
And thro' my veins with treacherous influence dart;
Inspire me, Heav'n! assist me, Grace divine,
Aid me, ye Saints! unknown to pains like mine;
You, who on earth serene all griefs could prove,
All but the tort'ring pangs of hopeless love;
A holier rage in your pure bosoms dwelt,
Nor can you pity what you never felt:
A sympathising grief alone can lure,
The hand that heals, must feel what I endure.
Thou, Eloise alone canst give me ease,
And bid my struggling soul subside to peace;
Restore me to my long lost heav'n of rest,
And take thyself from my reluctant breast;

If crimes like mine could an allay receive,
That blest allay thy wond'rons charms might give.
Thy form, that first to love my heart inclin'd,
Still wanders in my lost, my guilty mind.
I saw thee as the new blown blossoms fair,
Sprightly as light, more soft than summer's air,
Bright as their beams thy eyes a mind disclose,
Whilst on thy lips gay blush'd the fragrant rose;
Wit, youth, and love, in each dear feature shone;
Prest by my fate, I gaz'd—and was undone.
 There dy'd the gen'rous fire, whose vig'rous flame
Enlarged my soul, and urg'd me on to same;
Nor fame, nor wealth, my soften'd heart could move,
Dully insensible to all but love.
Snatch'd from myself, my learning tasteless grew;
Vain my philosophy, oppos'd to you;
A train of woes succeed, nor should we mourn,
The hours that cannot, ought not to return.
As once to love I sway'd your yielding mind,
Too fond, alas! too fatally inclin'd,
To virtue now let me your breast inspire,
And fan, with zeal divine, the heav'nly fire;
Teach you to injur'd Heav'n all chang'd to turn,
And bid the soul with sacred rapture burn.
O! that my own example might impart
This noble warmth to your soft trembling heart!
That mine, with pious undissembled care,
Could aid the latent virtue struggling there;
Alas! I rave—nor grace, nor zeal divine,
Burn in a heart oppress'd with crimes like mine,
Too sure I find, while I the tortures prove
Of feeble piety, conflicting love,
On black despair my forc'd devotion's built;
Absence for me has sharper pangs than guilt.
Yet, yet, my Eloisa, *thy charms I view,*
Yet my sighs breath, my tears pour forth for you;
Each weak resistance stronger knits my chain,
I sigh, weep, love, despair, repent——in vain,

Haste, Eloisa, haste, your lover free,
Amidst your warmest pray'r——O think on me!
Wing with your rising zeal my grov'ling mind,
And let me mine from your repentance find!
Ah! labour, strife, your love, your self control!
The change will sure affect my kindred soul;
In blest consent our purer sighs shall breath,
And Heav'n assisting, shall our crimes forgive,
But if unhappy, wretched, lost in vain,
Faintly th' unequal combat you sustain;
If not to Heav'n you feel your bosom rise,
Nor tears refin'd fall contrite from your eyes;
If still, your heart its wonted passions move,
If still, to speak all pains in one—you love;
Deaf to the weak essays of living breath,
Attend the stronger eloquence of Death.
When that kind pow'r this captive soul shall free,
Which only then can cease to doat on thee;
When gently sunk to my eternal sleep,
The Paraclete my peaceful urn shall keep!
Then, Eloisa, then your lover view,
See his quench'd eyes no longer gaze on you;
From their dead orbs that tender utt'rance flown,
Which first to thine my heart's soft fate made known,
This breast no more, at length to ease consign'd,
Pant like the waving aspin in the wind;
See all my wild, tumultuous passion o'er,
And thou, amazing change! belov'd no more;
Behold the destin'd end of human love——
But let the fight your zeal alone improve;
Let not your conscious soul, to sorrow mov'd,
Recall how much, how tenderly I lov'd:
With pious care your fruitless griefs restrain,
Nor let a tear your sacred veil profane;
Not ev'n a sigh on my cold urn bestow;
But let your breast with new-born raptures glow;
Let love divine, frail mortal love dethrone,
And to your mind immortal joys make known;

Let Heav'n relenting strike your ravish'd view,
And still the bright, the blest pursuit renew!
So with your crimes shall your misfortune cease,
And your rack'd soul be calmly hush'd to peace.

THE END